ANUNNAKI PRIESTESS
INSIDE A BABYLONIAN TEMPLE
NEW STANDARD ZUIST EDITION

POCKET EDITION

Published from the Joshua Free Imprint (JFI Publications)
Mardukite Borsippa HQ, San Luis Valley, Colorado
Founding Church of Mardukite Zuism,
Mardukite Academy & Systemology Society
for religious and educational purposes only.

ANUNNAKI PRIESTESS

INSIDE A BABYLONIAN TEMPLE

NEW STANDARD ZUIST EDITION

Project developed by Kyra Kaos
writing with Joshua Free for
The Church of Mardukite Zuism

THE JOSHUA FREE IMPRINT
JFI PUBLICATIONS

© 2025, JOSHUA FREE

ISBN : 978-1-961509-67-2

A special pocket version of the
previously unpublished text
for Mardukite Liber-P1;
an account of ancient Mesopotamian
religion from a modern-day practitioner
edited for founding the
Church of Mardukite Zuism

Pocket Paperback Edition — *July 2025*
mardukite.com

Discover What It Was Like To Serve In The _Original_ Temples on Planet Earth

TRUE INITIATION...

Learn the secrets of ancient Mesopotamian religion and the Anunnaki priesthood of Babylon as drawn from cuneiform tablets and revealed to all in the premiere of the first new addition to the "Mardukite Core" esoteric research library in nearly a decade.

Here is a fresh approach to understanding the Sumerian Anunnaki and Babylonian Religion, as given by an experienced modern-day High Priestess. Whether an adept or newcomer to this New Age vision for Mesopotamian Neopaganism, here is a concise practical guide detailing such topics as:

* Beliefs and Daily Life in Ancient Babylon
* Babylonian Anunnaki Gods and Goddesses
* Mesopotamian Priests, Priestesses and Temples
* Symbols, Tools and Magical Rules in Babylon
* Cuneiform Prayer Tablets, Hymns and Chants
* Rituals, Rites and Ceremonies of the Clergy

Experience a new perspective of Anunnaki tradition with this literary debut by Kyra Kaos, a long-standing Mardukite Academy instructor, writing with prolific author and Mardukite founder, Joshua Free. "Anunnaki Priestess" makes an excellent companion to "The Complete Anunnaki Bible" and related titles, including: "Anunnaki Gods," "Anunnaki History" and "Anunnaki Origins."

New Standard Zuist Editions (Pocket Library)

Anunnaki Bible – The Cuneiform Scriptures

Anunnaki Gods – The Sumerian Religion

Anunnaki Prayers – The Cuneiform Almanac

Anunnaki History – The Magic of Babylon

Anunnaki Origins – The Epic of Creation

Anunnaki Rites – The Maqlu Ritual Book

Anunnaki Priestess – Inside a Babylonian Temple

Anunnaki Wisdom – The Tablet of Destinies

What is Mardukite Zuism – The Power of Zu

TABLET OF CONTENTS

GENERAL INTRODUCTION TO THE NEW STANDARD ZUIST EDITION SERIES

The Mardukite Chamberlains (Mardukite Research Organization) completed its Year-1 cycle of work in early 2010—and those efforts culminated into an anthology first released as "*Necronomicon: The Anunnaki Bible*"—but which, for a recent solidification of our tradition as Mardukite Zuism, has also been published as "*The Complete Anunnaki Bible*"; and even a newly revised pocket-portable abridged format, "*Anunnaki Bible: The Cuneiform Scriptures (New Standard Zuist Edition)*," is available. That culmination of material has certainly earned its recognition as a critical staple and source book for a modern Mardukite revival, even now, well over a decade later.

Although a necessary foundation to work from, completion of the Year-1 (2009) work proved to be only a beginning for the route that would carry and build a global underground spiritual movement, now, into the 2020's and beyond with a revitalized "religious brand" as *Mardukite Zuism* and its very effective *Systemology* of applied spiritual technology. Much of this would not have been possible— or even coherently relevant—were it not for the pivotal Year-2 (2010) continuation of efforts made by "Chamberlains Alumni," those that dedicated another year of attention to the practical esoteric interpretation of the *"Anunnaki Bible"* and its background. And the "Mardukite Core" was born.

In 2010, we began publishing an extensive esoteric library to establish stronger foundations for a modern interest in reviving Mesopotamian traditions, particularly Babylonian. This included "Liber-50" (*"Sumerian Religion"*), "Liber-W" (*"The Book of Marduk by Nabu"*), "Liber-51" (*"Babylonian Myth & Magic"*) and "Liber-M" (*"Maqlu Ritual Book"*) —all of which we reissued as 10th Anniversary Collector's Edition hardcovers; all of which have been retitled and published as individual volumes of this *'New Standard Zuist Edition'* pocket series.

After nearly a decade of underground behind-the-scenes development by the Mardukite Org, the first advancement in *Mardukite Zuism* appeared in 2019—*"The Tablets of Destiny Revelation"* (Liber-One) which simultaneously presented the very first *Systemology Core Research Volume* to the public. Its original project title was *"Anunnaki Wisdom"*— and as such we now include it in this *NSZE* series. It is referenced several times in the *'Power of ZU'* lectures—transcripts of which are already published in this series as *"What is Mardukite Zuism."* Mostly, it is significant for the fact that it *bridges* ancient Mardukite wisdom *with* a futurist 'Nex-Gen' Mardukite Ascension movement known as Systemology—the pinnacle of which is now available as the *'New Standard Systemology'* volumes.

MARDUKITE

ZUISM

A BRIEF
INTRODUCTION

*According to the most ancient
historical records
written at the birth of our
modern civilization...*

432,000 YEARS AGO...*

a small population of advanced beings—called the <u>ANUNNAKI</u>—began developing the planet Earth for their purposes. These elite Self-Actualized spiritual beings resided on Earth in physical bodies, but found their forms inadequate for the physical labors required. Enter: the "Human Condition." Ancient "<u>cuneiform</u>" tablet writings from Sumerians and Babylonians of Mesopotamia are clear regarding the original creation and systematic programming of Humanity.

CUNEIFORM...

is the oldest known writing system used by scribes of ancient Babylon to record their wisdom and the history of humanity on <u>clay tablets</u>. "Cuneiform" is named for its style of wedge-shaped script formed by a <u>reed pen</u> called a "<u>stylus.</u>" Rather than an alphabet of letters, cuneiform is a system of "<u>signs</u>" representing "things" and "ideas." These may be combined to represent even more complex "signs."

---

*   Version 1.1 – First published in 2019 as "*Mardukite Zuism: A Brief Introduction*" in booklet format.

Many concepts adopted for modern "<u>Mardukite Zuism</u>" are derived from cuneiform tablets. The ANUNNAKI introduced complex writing systems in order to program civilization and all parameters of Reality for the Human Condition. Legendary "<u>Tablets of Destiny</u>" (Divine Truth, supreme knowledge and cosmic power of the "gods") were first introduced to Humanity in the Babylonian narrative known best as the "<u>Epic of Creation</u>.

THE ARCANE TABLETS.

Ancient Babylonians used the Tablets of Destiny & Creation Epic to systematize all cosmic knowledge into a workable <u>paradigm</u> called "Mardukite Zuism"—a <u>systemology</u> received directly from the ANUNNAKI.

> <u>Paradigm</u> : an all-encompassing standard or religion used to view the world and communicate reality.

> <u>Systemology</u> : applied philosophies of Mardukite Zuism combined with personal spiritual techniques and technology ("Tech") that is effectively demonstrating systematic principles of a "paradigm."

THE EPIC OF CREATION.

Seven cuneiform tablets compose the ancient Babylonian Epic of Creation, named the Enuma Eliš by scholars after its opening lines. These seven tablets are the basis for what later traditions refer to as the *"Seven Days of Creation."* The *Epic of Creation* tablets describe development of all existences with a Divine artistic perfection. The Enuma Eliš is the core example of religious literature from Babylon, which served as the basis for ancient *"Mardukite Zuism"*—the first true systematized religion in history.

THE SYSTEMOLOGY OF LIFE, UNIVERSES & EVERYTHING.

The *Arcane Tablets* describe the division of the ALL by the LAW, outside of which is but IN-FINITY. The *Epic of Creation* describes these activities as "mythology."

The Mardukite Systemology "Standard Model" uses the same information to demonstrates...

that <u>ALL</u> ("AN-KI") envelops both:
the <u>Spiritual Existences</u> ("AN")
and the <u>Physical Existences</u> ("KI")
divided by <u>Cosmic Law</u> and
connected by <u>Life-Awareness</u> ("ZU")
and beyond which is only the <u>Abyss</u>,
an <u>Infinity of Nothingness</u> ("ABZU").

ANCIENT SUMERIAN DEFINITIONS.

<u>ABZU</u> = "Abyss" ("Nothingness")
<u>ZU</u> = "Spiritual Life" ("Awareness")
<u>ANKI</u> = "All Existences" ("Existence")
<u>AN</u> = "Spiritual Universe" ("Heaven")
<u>KI</u> = "Physical Universe" ("Earth")

ALTERNATE MARDUKITE NEXGEN SYSTEMOLOGY DEFINITIONS.

<u>ABZU</u> = "Infinity of Nothingness"
<u>ZU</u> = "Awareness of Alpha Spirit"
<u>ANKI</u> = "The Standard Model"
<u>AN</u> = "Alpha Existence" ("Spiritual")
<u>KI</u> = "Beta Existence" ("Physical")

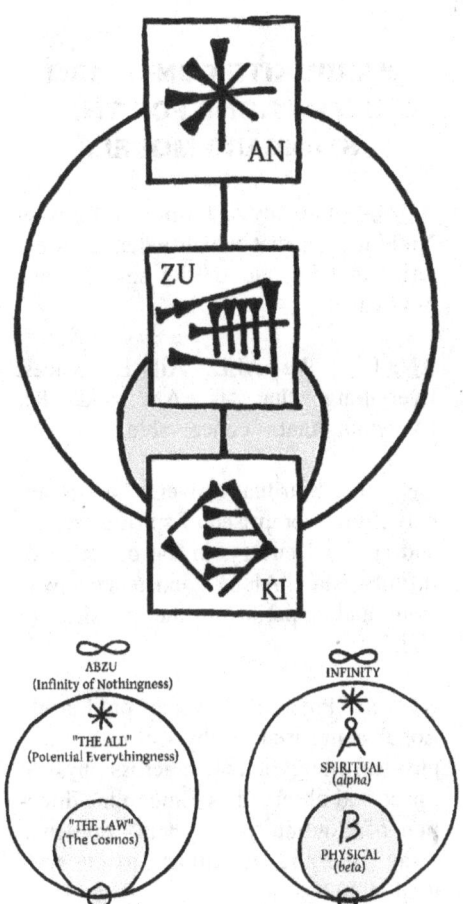

AN

ZU

KI

∞
ABZU
(Infinity of Nothingness)

✳
"THE ALL"
(Potential Everythingness)

"THE LAW"
(The Cosmos)

∞
INFINITY

✳
Å
SPIRITUAL
(alpha)

β
PHYSICAL
(beta)

MARDUKITE CUNEIFORM DEFINITIONS FOR THE STANDARD MODEL.

<u>ABZU</u> = the Abyss; Infinity; Infinity of Nothingness; that which extends, is exterior and beyond of the spiritual and physical.

<u>ANKI</u> = the ALL; All Existences; Everything that is AN and KI; Everything that is conceivable.

<u>AN</u> = the "Spiritual Universe" or "Heavenly Zone" comprised of spiritual matter and spiritual energy, in the direction of Infinity—an "Alpha" existence away from and superior to the physical or "KI."

<u>KI</u> = the "Physical Universe" or "Earthly Zone" comprised of physical matter and physical energy in action across physical Space and observed as Time in the direction of Continuity—a "Beta" existence away from and subordinate to the spiritual or "AN."

<u>ZU</u> = "to know"; "knowingness"; "Awareness" or "consciousness"; spiritual energy and matter of AN that is observed as "Lifeforce" in KI; "Spiritual Life Energy"; the actual personal spiritual Identity or "Awareness" of Self as Spirit which extends along a "line" from the Spiritual Universe (AN) to the Physical Universe (KI).

THE TABLETS OF DESTINY & BABYLONIAN CREATION EPIC.

The Absolute behind ALL Existence is referred to on the *Tablets of Destiny* as the Infinity of Nothingness. It is the only constant static of latent unmanifest potentiality of ALL and Everythingness.

The LAW—Cosmic Law—is defined as the Cosmic Dragon—TIAMAT—on "Epic of Creation" Tablets. She is the First Cause or movement across a "Sea of Infinity." Later, the LAW becomes a division between Spiritual Existence ("AN") and any Physical Universe ("KI"). The LAW—Tiamat—permeating ALL, uses the *Tablets of Destiny* and then fixes the systems of finite potential: The Systems of Manifestation—Substance, Motion and Awareness.

"Before heaven or earth are named," the formation and interaction of active existences —"substances" and "bodies" and "Life" and "gods"—creates turbulence and waves of action through space. The governing system of Cosmic Law—Tiamat—responds accordingly. She fixes the Tablets of Destiny to her "deputy"—a messenger wave action of the LAW named "Kingu" and sends him rippling out to "meet" the Anunnaki "gods."

The Anunnaki Assembly of "gods" prepare to battle The LAW. When none among them comes forth to engage, it is the Anunnaki "god" MARDUK that volunteers as hero to confront Kingu and Tiamat—but with a condition that the Anunnaki Assembly recognize him as "Chief of the Gods" upon his success.

When MARDUK approaches the LAW directly, he is flanked by Kingu and the "army of Ancient Ones." MARDUK is able to relinquish the Tablets of Destiny from Kingu. With the Tablets of Destiny, Marduk conquers a true understanding of Cosmic Law and thereby Tiamat.

THE TABLETS OF DESTINY
& SELF-HONESTY.

Marduk uses the Tablets of Destiny to discover "Self-Honesty" and Divine Knowledge governing "Cosmic Ordering"—systems dividing the "Spiritual Universe" (AN) from a "Physical Universe" (KI). The two universes are connected only by a stream of Spiritual Lifeforce Awareness that Sumerians called ZU. Wisdom from the Arcane Tablets is later passed down to and concealed by an ancient esoteric secret society in Babylon: the Scribes, High Priests and Priestesses of Mardukite Zuism.

Self-Honesty is a term describing an original "Alpha" state of clear knowingness and Self-directed beingness. "Self-Honesty" is the most basic and true expression of Self as "I-AM"—free of artificial attachments; reactive-response conditioning; and imposed or enforced programming as Reality for the Human Condition. Spiritual development in modern *Mardukite Zuism* is referred to as the "Pathway to Self-Honesty" and the "Gateway to Infinity." It is modeled directly from the Ancient Mystery Tradition observed at the Temples of Babylon.

THE KEY TO THE GATE.

"I will take my Blood—and with Bone—I will fashion a Race of Humans to keep Watch of the Gate. And from the Blood of Kingu I will create another Race of Humans to inhabit the Earth in service to the Gods—so shrines to the Anunnaki may be built and the temples filled. I will bind the Elder Gods to the Watchtowers; let them keep watch over the Gate of Abzu and the Gate of Tiamat and Gate of Kingu—and with a Key that shall be ever hidden, known to none, except only to my Mardukites." —MARDUK, *Enuma Elis, Creation Tablet VI.*

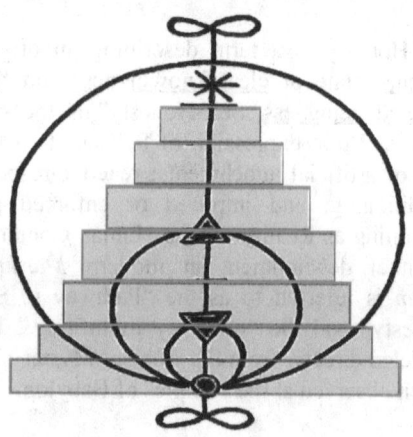

THE ANUNNAKI LADDER OF LIGHTS & BABYLONIAN GATEWAYS TO INFINITY.

ZIGGURAT TEMPLES in Babylonia—and throughout Mesopotamia—served to remind populations of the ZU connecting "Heaven" and "Earth."

Seven-stepped "levels" of the physical ZIG-GURAT TEMPLES of Babylonia—and seven corresponding Gates—represent spiritual levels of actualized Awareness; states of Self-purifica-tion (or "spiritual defragmentation") as they ascend in the direction of AN toward Infinity of Supreme Beingness—the Pathway of Self-Hon-esty—in imitation of the footsteps of the gods during their descent through the "spheres" or "Gates."

COSMOLOGY AND METAPHYSICS.

All Things in the Physical Universe are in mo-tion—wave motions of "energy and matter in space measured as-and-across time." Continuity of the Physical Universe (KI) is divided by LAW and encompassed by the ALL (ANKI).

The direction of AN extends toward ABZU, an Infinity of Nothingness beyond effective existence.

The true <u>Alpha Self</u> is a source—the "spiritual cause" of "physical effects." It engages a <u>Self-determined WILL</u> from its "spiritual" <u>Alpha existence</u> to actualize Awareness for "physical" <u>Beta existence</u> experience as "Life."

USING ANCIENT WISDOM TO UNLOCK HUMAN POTENTIAL.

Communication of clear wisdom and true knowledge from Arcane Tablets is distorted as it passes through time and geography, diverse languages and authoritarian cultures using the "Power" to program the masses and fragment the Human Condition away from Self-Honesty.

Use of this ancient wisdom reveals the Keys to "<u>Cosmic Ordering</u>"—applying the highest Self-directed understanding of "cause-and-effect" sequences in the Physical Universe.

MARDUKITE ZUISM, SYSTEMOLOGY & SPIRITUALITY.

The Spiritual Universe (AN)—of metaphysical or spiritual energy and metaphysical or spiritual matter is not dependent on the Physical Universe (KI) to exist; the two are existentially independent of each other, maintaining a single channel, conduit or connection, which is Alpha Spirit "Awareness" as Spiritual Life or ZU. The Alpha Spirit engages a ZU-line, a spiritual lifeline of ZU energy to a genetic vehicle or organic body to experience physical beta existence.

MARDUKITE ZUISM DEFINITIONS FOR SYSTEMOLOGY.

ALPHA SPIRIT = a spiritual lifeform; the True Self or "I-AM"; the spirit that is controlling the physical body or "genetic vehicle" using a Lifeline or continuum of spiritual "ZU" energy.

ASCENSION = actualized Awareness elevated to (AN) spiritual existence that is exterior to beta-existence.

BETA-EXISTENCE = manifestation in the Physical Universe (KI); the state of existence or condition of frequency specific to physical energy and physical matter in physical space.

FRAGMENTATION = breaking into parts; fractioning wholeness; fracture of holism; discontinuity; separation; outside the state of Self-Honesty.

GENETIC VEHICLE = a physical lifeform; the physical (beta) body controlled by the (Alpha) Spirit using a continuous Lifeline of ZU energy.

HUMAN CONDITION = a default programmed conditioned state standard issue Human existence/experience.

ZU-LINE = a spectrum of Spiritual Life-Energy (ZU); an energetic channel or Identity-Continuum connecting Alpha Spirit Awareness from Infinity-to-Infinity including the full physical beta range.

THE HIGHEST FORM OF
TRUE DIVINE WORSHIP.

The true Destiny of Humanity is to achieve spiritual <u>Self-Actualization</u>; the reunion of Self with the Divine. Attaining Self-Honesty in this Life is the most important step a person can take toward achieving their highest ideals, goals and realizations.

The Highest form of "True Worship" begins with the Spirit—the true Self—and all external practices, rituals, ceremonies and historical examples are but outer reflections of this ideal. The Highest form of "Sin" is against the Spirit —against the Self—and its ability to maintain Self-Honesty. There are modes of thought, action and Self-direction of effort that will contribute toward Ascension; and modes that lead away from that.

Beta experiences of "Sin"—pain, fear, guilt, anger—are all related to personal fragmentation; and emotional turbulence from all of these may be released—and intention energy redirected— because: <u>we are all co-creators of Reality in this lifetime!</u>

SPHERES OF EXISTENCE, INFLUENCE & UTILITARIAN ETHICS OF SYSTEMOLOGY.

The prime directive of all beta existence is: *to exist*. The continuation of existence is the purpose behind all existence. Between realization of Self and Infinity, there are many spheres of existence that we may influence. All of the spheres are interconnected.

There is nothing in existence that is in absolute exclusion to all existence. Each sphere of existence supports subsequent existences and assists reaches toward higher spheres of influence.

The greatest good contributes to the greatest continuation of optimum existence for the greatest sphere of inclusion. Degrees of rightness and wrongness are determined by Cosmic Law and are reflected in the quality of, and continuation of, an optimal existence at the highest sphere of existence.

Individual happiness is attained via the channel to the highest sphere. Human unhappiness is the result of "selfishness" and/or lack of "spiritual Self-Actualization" and "Awareness."

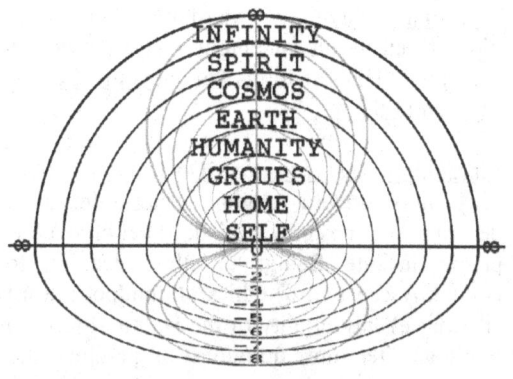

INFINITY
SPIRIT
COSMOS
EARTH
HUMANITY
GROUPS
HOME
SELF

ZU : MARDUKITE ZUISM & MODERN ZUIST RELIGION.

History demonstrates how dangerous, trouble-some and easily misused the concept of "REL-GION" is; so, for purposes of incorporating Mardukite Zuism as a contemporary standard, the idea of "religion" is here treated as:

> a concise spiritual paradigm, set of be-liefs and practices, regarding Divinity, Infinite Beingness—or else "God."

Mardukite Zuism operates under a premise of very specific beliefs and a "systemology" of "spiritual technology." Mardukite Zuist Religious Doctrine fundamentally relays previously described "Highest forms" of Worship, Cosmic Law, and Ethics.

Mardukite Zuist Spiritual Doctrines successfully meet modern religious criteria for: a) a description of cosmic creation; b) belief in a Supreme Infinite Being; c) ethics leading to Human Ascension; d) ethics of conduct toward all Life; e) Immortality of the Human Spirit; f) religious literature, traditions of practice and spiritual advisement.

GOALS & IDEALS OF MARDUKITE ZUISM.

The word "ZU" meant "knowing" in original Sumerian cuneiform script. Goals and ideals of Zuism reflect this. Mardukite Zuism seeks to assist an individual in reclaiming a realization of the True Self or "I-AM" as the Immortal Spirit, in line with a most ancient directive: to "Know Thyself."

In view of the fact that all modern humans are subjected to technologies depriving them of their freedoms to *be*, *think*, *know* and pursue truth: the goals and ideals of Zuism are to effectively revive and repair these very abilities and certainties of the Individual—as an increase of "Actualized Awareness."

INFINITY, "GOD" & SUPREME BEINGNESS

The Spiritual Philosophy of Zuism is systematized by a Standard Model. It demonstrates Absolute Supreme Beingness associated with the Highest realization of "God" as INFINITY. No thing is Higher or Absolute than the Infinity of Nothing—and reducing Supreme Beingness to any finite personality or character trait is to limit and defile with lesser "words."

The Highest Name of God cannot be conceived —hence our symbolic use of the Infinity Sign:

...or Sumerian cuneiform word-sign: "ABZU" —"The Infinite Nothingness and Source of All ZU."

The Spiritual Universe (AN) is *All-as-One* because it exists as an infinite singularity or stasis:

infinite potential with no gradient or observed motion; which is its own continuity.

The Physical Universe (KI) is *All-as-One* because it is in continuous motion, with all manifest parts working systematically as a continuity of beta-existence.

A "spiritual continuum" or "conduit channel" of ZU—absolute energy from the Spiritual Universe (AN)—links our Awareness levels of "I-AM," "True Self" or Spirit ("Alpha Spirit") with the degrees of motion and variation in the Physical Universe.

This Alpha Spirit or "Soul" is the true Awareness, "I" or "Self" connected to the operation and control of the physical body.

THE TRUE HUMAN ALPHA SPIRIT.

The true Self is the "I" or "Spirit" regardless of its position, degree or level of Awareness. Spirit remains. Whatever "spiritual energy-matter" composes the Alpha Spirit or "soul"—it must occupy this "other space" with its spiritual existence and then project its Awareness and Will onto the Physical Universe (KI) in order to experience the Game we call Life.

This "spiritual energy-matter" that composes all Life (as a Lifeforce with Awareness and Consciousness) goes by many names throughout history—but we find the idea first treated as ZU on cuneiform tablets of Mesopotamia.

On an Identity lifeline of ZU energy, all Alpha Spirits are operating from a Spiritual Universe. We refer to this as the ZU-line on the Standard Model.

ZU is the name given to the spiritual essence of all Life in existence—and Self is a concentrated center or focal point as a ZU-continuum or Identity.

The True Self of an Individual Human is a "spiritual universe cause" of "physical universe effects"—engaging as an immortal Alpha Spirit with a Self-determined Will actualized as an Awareness along the ZU-continuum, extending from Infinity-to-Infinity, through every possible frequency and vibration along the total spectrum of physical and metaphysical existence.

THE SYSTEMOLOGY PRACTICES OF SPIRITUAL ADVISEMENT & COUNSELING SERVICES FOR MARDUKITE ZUISM.

The Mardukite Chamberlains were established in 2009 dedicated to recovery and consolidation of all historical, scriptural & ritual records of ancient Babylon in Mesopotamia. In 2011, a Mardukite faction (International Systemology Society) began to research and develop methods to apply ancient wisdom as a futurist spiritual technology that awakens, unlocks and fully actualizes spiritual potential of the Human Condition.

A systematic approach to spirituality is seen on the Standard Model, where ZU-line frequencies are represented at various degrees: "zero-point" body death; cellular activity and sensory perceptions of a genetic body; bio-chemicals induced by emotion; thoughts and intention transmitted between our Alpha Spirit and the "genetic vehicle"—all the way "up" the scale to a perfected clarity of Self-Actualized Awareness of I-AM as our true "Alpha" state, just below Infinity and Absolute Beingness.Full potential of ZU in Consciousness is only altered from its natural state as a result of personal fragmentation of the Human Condition. This may be restored with spiritual practices.

The Pathway to Self-Honesty is a personal journey and spiritual adventure marked by progressive clearing of spiritual energy channels fragmented by the imprinting and programming accumulated from experiences in our environment—the "debris" that fragments the total actualized experience of Self in Awareness as the Alpha Spirit.

The first and most important step—Before an individual can actualize potentials of the Spirit as Self, they must fully realize: the I-AM Self and the Alpha Spirit are One.

This state of Knowingness is the primary intention of basic spiritual practices found in Mardukite Zuism.

"Systemology" books and advanced training courses are also available to Mardukite Ministers seeking to qualify as specialized clergy, priests, priestess, and systematic processing pilots.

CREED OF MARDUKITE ZUISM.
PRINCIPLES OF BELIEF.[*]

1.) We believe in an Absolute Beingness, which is Infinite—the ABZU—the All-as-One encompassing Source of All Being, Knowing and Awareness to all Alpha (Spiritual-AN) and Beta (Physical-KI) states of existence.

2.) We believe in a spiritual energy of all Life and Awareness—ZU—in the physical universe (beta) that is an effect of a spiritual (Alpha) cause; a Spirit that is cause. This Spirit—in its Alpha state—is the True Self "I-AM" Individual Identity that many have called the "soul."

3.) We believe that the Human Condition is a genetic vehicle used by a spiritual source (AN) to experience the Finite as physical existence (KI)—that we are Awareness (ZU) projected onto a genetic vehicle—and that while the vehicle/body may perish to physical entropy, the "Alpha Spirit" remains immortal and Self-directed to the extent of its own Actualized Awareness.

---

[*]   First drafted in 2019.

4.) We believe that the highest form of worship and spirituality is the actualization and advancement of our "Self" as Spirit in Self-Honesty—and that Self-Honesty is the I-AM Alpha state of Being and Knowing, which is realizable in this lifetime.

5.) We believe that the purpose of all existence is: to exist—and that the prime directive of all spiritual Life is: continued existence of spiritual Life and co-creation of habitable Reality. "Good" and "Moral" actions are evaluated to the extent of this end.

6A.) We believe that no Life exists in exclusion to all other Life—and that the conditions of a habitable Reality extending from Self include:
Home; Community; All Humanity; All Life on Earth; All Life in the Universe; All Spiritual Life; and the Infinite.

6B.) We believe in a continued evolution of Alpha Spirit awareness developed beyond one physical life, and that a Spirit experiences many.

7A.) We believe Mardukite Zuism and its applied systemology is a 21st Century AD synthesis of the 21st Century BC wisdom collected on cuneiform tablets and experienced in ancient Mesopotamia, esp. Babylon.

7B.) This cuneiform library included details concerning: beings called the Anunnaki; ordering of the Cosmos; creation of Humanity; and an entire legacy of systematized traditions.

8.) We believe in the continuation of, and proper communication of, the true legacy of Human history—and the ability of every Human to realize that they are a Free Spirit in a Free Zone of Self-Determinism: and no "evils" can affect intentions if an individual is spiritually Self-Actualized in Self-Honesty.

THE ARCANE KNOWLEDGE FROM
MARDUK'S TABLET OF DESTINY.*

1.) As above, so below;
On earth as it is in Heaven
an-bala ki-bala an-ba ki an-ba

2.) What the Mind believes, the Spirit reinforces
da-ga nam-ku-zu dingir-Lamma a bi-ib-gar

3.) When disaster is self-made,
no man can interfere
*nig-ku-lam-ma dingir-ra-na-ka su—
tu-tu nu-ub-zu*

4.) What is given in submission
is a catalyst for defiance
nig-gu-gar-ra nig-gaba-gar-ra

5.) Whoever partners with Truth, creates Life
nig-ge-na-ta a-ba in-da-di nam-ti i-u-tu

---

* From *"Tablets of Destiny (Revelation)"* by Joshua Free.

PRIESTESS OF

BABYLON

(LIBER-P1)

ORIGINAL FOREWORD TO "LIBER-P1"

by Joshua Free

When we published "*The Tablets of Destiny Revelation*" in late *2019*, the emphasis of the *Mardukite Research Org* became almost exclusively dedicated to research and development for titles composing the '*Systemology Esoteric Research Library*'. I had already considered my previous work for the '*Mardukite Core Research Library*' completed. But, Kyra's notebook demonstrated that there were still quite a few holes in our existing communication that needed to be filled for modern practitioners. We originally planned to publish "*Priestess of Babylon*" in late *2021*, when Kyra brought me the first draft of this highly anticipated work. Needless to say, after being "lost in the shuffle" for quite a while, its appearance now in book form is long overdue.

This current volume does not replace knowledge gained from other '*Mardukite Core*' titles. It supplements anything a *Seeker* has already learned quite well. In that same 'spirit', but with newcomers in mind, I have added appropriate details to Kyra's original outline that will make this material even more accessible for those that haven't already studied anything of our existing '*Core*'. And to clarify, I should point out here that by '*Mardukite Core*', we mean specifically the material found in '*The Complete Anunnaki Bible*', '*Sumerian Religion*', '*Babylonian Myth & Magic*', and even '*The Tablets of Destiny Revelation*' (all of which are also available as alternate titles for the '*New Standard Zuist Edition*' series).

Many ancient cultures and esoteric traditions have experienced revival attention and reconstructionist efforts, popularly extending back even to the *Egyptians*. Yet, what is to be found concerning the "mother-of-them-all," *Mesopotamia*, the *Sumerians*, and especially the bold beauty and richness that is *Babylon*? To fill this need and provide answers for the New Age, I founded "*Mardukite Ministries*" (*Mardukite Zuism*) and the *Mardukite Research Org* in *2008*. This pursuit led me directly to start developing our unique "*Systemology*" a decade later, which is the main emphasis of the *Mardukite Academy* today—but the earlier fundamentals uncovered from *arcane tablets* in the *ancient Near East* cannot be easily dismissed. And even today, in *2025*, the modern *Mardukite* legacy propagated from those original efforts, now *seventeen years* later, has remained—and it continues to reach thousands of new *Seekers* each year.

For all intents and purposes, the modern *Mardukite* effort is a living legacy that still has room for inclusion. In this case, for this book, we are opening the arms of our '*esoteric library*' to allow for a new addition—*Liber-P1*—the first new official addition to the '*Mardukite Core*' in nearly a decade. Those seeking to better understand ancient practices of Babylonian Tradition and the role of Anunnaki Priestesses (and other clergy) of the Temple Priesthood in ancient Babylon will certainly not be disappointed. Those seeking to enrich their own personal New Age tradition will find a genuine source of inspiration here. So, *be inspired and create!*

—Joshua Free, "Nabu"
Mardukite Founder
Mardukite Borsippa HQ
May's Eve 2025

ORIGINAL INTRODUCTION TO "LIBER-P1"

by Kyra Kaos

When I started keeping literary records of my "Mardukite" journey, now almost a decade ago, I did not realize what a long and strange trip it would become. What began with a random chance meeting in Chicago resulted or manifested as the critical starting point of my *"aware life"*—kicking off of esoteric studies allowing me to more widely *awaken* into a world, both *real* and *fantastical*, which previously I had only gleaned brief tears of when mentioned by others. But really, a world that I had only dreamed of being *real*. A world where faeries, wizards, and magic actually exist; where energy itself is utilized for shaping reality—and that I could do this *knowingly*, or that I had already been participating in creating reality *unknowingly*. This recognition, or rediscovered ability of "creation" or manifestation into the physical, sparked like fireworks within me, shining light on the *"unknown"* and the (perhaps purposely for whatever reasons) *forgotten*.

While passing through Chicago on my way elsewhere, I quite unexpectedly had a chance run-in with a prolific writer who was also just passing through. Within a short time, *Joshua Free* introduced me to his *many* literary works, which covered *many* areas or topics—yet, I found his almost omniscient advice on one subject in particular led me curiously into the heart of *THE* ancient city of *Babylon*, called 'City of the Lords', 'City of Star-Lights', 'City of the Gates' and 'City of the Gods'.

I do not recollect a single public school lesson regarding *Mesopotamia*—the "cradle of civilization" (as many academicians refer to it today). Yet there it *is*—or *was*—the "birthplace" of the 'systems' of 'civilized' society. And so, alongside (and inherent in) my efforts to learn magic and study systemology, I was privileged to find what I believed to be the *oldest*—the *beginning*—tradition and magic from the brief time when the *Gods* deigned to physically "come down" and personally visit planet Earth, intermingling with the results of their creations; when the *Gods* roamed the lands, their very presence witnessed by humans—something appearing very *solid* and *real* to them, rather than only being able to worship idols on altars and phantoms from afar.

Unfortunately, that once *real* and *physical* presence has been visibly absent from our view since a time when the walls of Babylon still stood. But those walls eventually disappeared as well. So much of the evidence to support this present work has long since passed into obscurity, leaving most folks today with little more than shadowy legends to behold when we speak of Mesopotamia, Babylon, the Anunnaki, or Sumerians. Today we must rely on fractured statues and even more highly fragmented *"cuneiform tablet writings"* in which to base our work. But what remains *are* the remains of the *original*, the *oldest*, and that which later cultures and traditions based their own beliefs and divine pantheons on. And if nothing else, for that reason, this all seemed very important. So, I decided to 'kill two birds with one stone' (as they say) and study the oldest magical religion while simultaneously compiling a notebook of my studies. It has taken some time, but here finally is my own direct contribution to further the data collected in the *Mardukite Research Library*.

This book is for *you*—it is *not just* for "females" or "aspiring priestesses." Really, this book is for *everyone*—not just for those who have already reached advanced studies regarding Mesopotamia and/or other Mardukite Zuism publications (on Babylonian Tradition). Although there are certainly more *details* available that are not contained within these pages, all of the critical basics are here—meaning, the basis for a solid understanding is provided here—in a series of chapter-lessons incrementally progressing, building upon each other, without unnecessarily over-complicating this subject-matter for newcomers.

In the first chapter, I introduce you to the core beliefs of a Babylonian, as well as their culture and daily life. The second chapter concerns the Babylonian pantheon, Anunnaki gods and goddesses, and some of their cult cities. The third chapter is specifically about priestesses and other information about clergy serving the temple priesthood.

The fourth chapter describes various symbols, tools, and basic rules regarding practice of Mesopotamian "religious magic" as once used in Babylon. The fifth chapter gives examples of prayers, chants, and hymns—and this is studied prior to the sixth chapter on rites, rituals, and incantations. Combined these are meant to setup a suitable understanding that allows you to create your own unique modern-day "tradition"—a tradition that is both personally relevant to you and historically authentic. This book closes with a bonus chapter and appendix that I will let you discover on your own.

In the ancient temples of the Gods, the priestesses were *Earthborn* females, *initiated* in the ways of the sacred arts. They were individually selected from all across the known world and dispatched to temples, learning of what is *known* and *unknown* alike; and how to properly serve the gods and goddesses as nationally recognized intermediaries, working both for the people and the deity they wished to communicate with—serving as a religious and political bridge between the mundane world and the divine.

Priestesses received offerings and petitions from the people to give to the deities, then relayed their divine wisdom and responses in return. The truth behind this method of worship has all but disappeared from the religions and traditions in practice during this modern age. We have lost communication with the divine. Should you wish to reclaim what was lost: a pathway in that direction begins here. And as you are already an *Earthborn* human (or not—*it's okay, we won't tell...*) then, the next step to entering the secret priesthood is a *true initiation*—a learning experience that pertains to specially selected materials and texts arranged for study to bring you all the information you will need to get you well on your way.

The knowledge of life, the gods,
   and everything is at your fingertips.
     But, remember: Life is a game.
     So, have fun with it.

—*Kyra "Light" Kaos*
High Priestess
Mardukite Babylon
March 2025

⁑ 1 ⁑
BELIEFS AND DAILY LIFE
IN BABYLON

*"The education of the Babylonians was entirely in
the hands of the priesthood, who derived their
knowledge from Nabu, the inventor of writing and
letters, and every kind of learning—the Lord of the
Houses of Tablets (or books), i.e. the first libraries."*
—E.A. Wallis Budge, Babylonian Life & History

ANCIENT MESOPOTAMIAN RELIGION

The Sumerians cultivated the earliest recorded
roots of our own modern civilization in prehistoric
Mesopotamia, approximately six-thousand years
ago. We consider those first origins "prehistoric"
because they predate "history." As noted Sumeri-
ologist, Samuel Kramer, was fond of saying:
"history begins in Sumer." It is in Mesopotamia
where "history"—which is to say, "definitive written records accounting for human activity"—is
first chronicled and archived, using *cuneiform*, the
first true "writing system." Some of these writings
(known as the *King-Lists*) also suggest prior *Anunnaki** activity on Earth for approximately 500,000

---

* *Anunnaki* — a Mesopotamian word for a race of
   "*Gods*" (possibly "*StarGods*") that once walked
   upon the Earth (and inspired a diverse number of

years, but for whatever reasons, our "modern" civilization required a deliberate and systematic "restart" in Mesopotamia around 4000 BCE.

The *Mardukite* "Anunnaki" tradition (both ancient and modern) that is emphasized in this book specifically concerns the beliefs, culture, and daily life of the *Babylonians*. There are, however, many instances where languages overlap—and earlier *Sumerian* words are retained in later *Babylonian* traditions. This book approaches this subject from the feminine perspective (as a "*priestess*") with an emphasis that differs from most other modern *Mardukite* publications (authored solely by Joshua Free).

Historically, the Old-Babylonian tradition is a amalgamation of *Akkadian* (northern Mesopotamia) and *Sumerian* (southern Mesopotamia) cultures, which were began in *c.* 2150 BCE. By the time of the infamous Hammurabi, *Babylon* had become the capital city-state of a singular Mesopotamian empire, led by an *Amorite* (proto-*Mardukite*) King. Over a thousand years later, the original *Mardukite* tradition was revitalized again under another famous king, Nebuchadnezzar II, who oversaw the Neo-Babylonian Renaissance era.

Generally speaking, the ancient Mesopotamians

---

religious mythologies in many other cultures) under many different names.

were responsible for many "firsts" that are still with us today; many essential staples of "civilization" that we might dismissively take for granted. In spite of the thousands of years that have passed, many elements of the ancient world are eerily similar to our own. This makes it easier for a student of history to study and understand the most visible surface elements. Yet if we wanted to recreate a exact duplication, "reconstruction" or "revival" of the tradition today, some major differences might prevent this:

1. <u>Religion</u>: the main focus of Babylonian society
   – and –
2. <u>Geography</u>: being ancient Mesopotamia

Religion prompted development of the very first *city-states*, each spreading out around a large "temple-shrine" to a particular Anunnaki deity. Long before organized warfare required the need for military-chieftains or warlord-kings, civilization was originally governed by the Temple high-priest (*en*) and high-priestess (*entu*). A definitive presence of the "Gods" and the power bestowed to their intermediary clergy dominated the everyday considerations of the ancient "citizens" residing within the city-walls.

Though abstract worship does play some small role in modern-day life, a true and pure belief system is no longer the life-blood of civilization. People may go to church and celebrate religious

traditions just to satisfy some social expectation—
or because "it's just what you're supposed to do."
But, we no longer live in the "Age of Gods." And
we certainly do not privately live and act as
though we are under the scrutiny of an ever-watch-
ful eye from above. As the ages shifted in
Babylon, when only the temple-statues remained
in the shrines (in the absence of "Living Gods"), a
residual resonance still lingered, even if only a
shadow of what had been—a physically solid
memory instead of a intangible ghost.

Now, touching on location, geography, time and
space: we obviously do not live in the alluvial
deserts of ancient Babylon. This is important because *environment* is a key factor that determined
what an ancient Mesopotamian could *do* and *how*
they lived. New innovation frequently sprung from
necessity. For example: where today eyeshadow
and liner is used as a fashion statement, in
Babylon (as in Egypt), black kohl served to keep
the scorching glare of an unforgiving sun from
one's eyes.

Southern Mesopotamia—the once fertile region of
Babylon—offered plenty of water and rich soils,
but few other natural resources. *Culture* was the
real influential export from this region. Nearly
everything else had to be imported from elsewhere. Large blocks of stone, such as used by
Egyptians for pyramid-building, were unavailable.

It has been said that not even a pebble existed there that was not carried from an outside source. Babylonians relied on their ability to extract *clay* from the land—and *bitumen,* a unique natural-springing asphalt that could adhere clay-bricks and provide waterproof coatings.

Since Mesopotamia enjoyed an agricultural and textile abundance, a new social role—the *merchant*—arose, someone to manage foreign trade routes of overland caravans and cargo-boats. As populations grew larger and more prosperous, and its rulers sought greater architectural splendor for their nation, additional resources and sturdier building materials were imported from surrounding countries. The *lapis lazuli* stone famously interwoven throughout Babylonia was actually imported from Afghanistan. All lumber came from Lebanon or the Zagros Mountains—especially since the local *date palm* was much more valuable alive for its fruit than as wood. Any precious metals had to be brought in from as far as Anatolia, Egypt, and the Indus River Valley.

Basic *environmental* factors not only affected attainable resources, but also shaped *social* culture and religious tones. In the fertile river-flowing desert plains of Mesopotamia (as with Egypt), the *"Waters of Life"* are treated as spiritually superior. Properly handling the "water element" (*e.g.* *irrigation*) is what made life in Babylon possible. In fact, once when the rivers were maliciously kept from flowing in Babylon for a time (as recorded on the *Erra Epos* tablets), its nation nearly collapsed into ruin. But this all contrasts greatly with cultures from colder environments further north that treat the "*Sacred Fire*" more centrally in their traditions. Essentially, the thing a society lacks (or needs most) to survive is what gets *prayed for*. The order of importances and beliefs then shapes what becomes national religion.

We'll begin this chapter by displaying a list of some of the more basic beliefs and values (or themes) fundamental to Babylonian society. Then, for those seeking greater depth from their studies: we offer a simple activity with a few short questions to start you on your way.

BELIEFS, VALUES & THEMES

1. **THE WILL OF THE GODS IS MANIFEST IN NATURE AND SKILL.** *This gives insight into their will.*

2. **SERVICE OF THE GODS IS HUMANITY'S PRIMARY FUNCTION.** *The Gods domesticated (civilized) humans for their own purposes; also teaching them to maintain the waterways, agriculture and infrastructure that would perpetually support said civilization (domestication).*

3. **"WHATEVER WAS PURE, WAS PURE AS LIGHT. WHATEVER WAS PURE, WAS BRIGHT."** *In spite of the shadowy gloom that often enshrouds portrayals of Mesopotamia, the Babylonians sought the 'Light' and revered 'bright' things. This is evident by religiously emphasizing an 'illumination of truth' by the Sun and 'radiance' of the Moon—and naming all the celestial lights observed in the night sky after their Gods.*

4. **IMPURITY IS SPREAD FROM PLACE TO PLACE.** *Words and ideas travel organically, as does pestilence and disease.*

5. **TRUE WISDOM.** *The earliest influential wisdom traditions—predating Greece, the Far East, and even Egypt—migrated out from Mesopotamia. Living the "Right Way" meant observing the will of the Gods, which is to say "Cosmic Law."*

6. **COMMUNITY DYNAMICS.** *A happy, healthy, prosperous, progressive, actualized community (society) is composed of many happy, healthy, prosperous, productive, actualized family units (households), which are composed of happy, healthy, productive, progressive, actualized individuals. Thus, self-actualized individuals are required for a strong healthy community.*

7. INTUITION. *The "Right Way" for an individual is that path which allows the True Self—or Personal Spirit—to properly unfold and be recognized. In modern pop-psychology, this might be reduced to the idea of embracing one's "shadow" or "inner child"— but at a higher level, true intuition is accessible only when the filters are removed that prevent the Spiritual Self from knowing itself.*

8. HOSPITALITY. *Traditionally, one was always accommodating to a guest (unless given a reason otherwise). Faithful reciprocation generally also prevailed; which at another level, led to standardizing trade.*

9. LOVE. *Among the diverse cuneiform tablets unearthed from the sands we find the oldest records of love songs, romantic poetry, and even quite colorful and explicit erotica. Ancient writers were also not shy about detailing the relationship drama and sexual exploits of the Anunnaki Gods.*

10. CREATIVITY. *Systematization and agriculture established the basis for civilization and replaced the nomadic hunter-gatherer lifestyle that kept prehistoric humans completely preoccupied with basic survival. As a result, true "culture" was born—one that embraced creativity inherent in the arts, music and poetry. This is evident in the design of pottery* *and jewelry dating as far back as the fourth millennium B.C.E., and depicting ornate spirals and knots closely resembling that of the Celts thousands of years later.*

11. **MAGIC.** *Babylonian clergy and wise-ones held a dualistic understanding of the cosmos (creation). They observed a relationship between two distinct states: the "Here" (the physical, the Earth, matter) and the "Other"—that visible things "seen" are propagated and perturbed by what is relatively "unseen." At a higher level, "magic" involved understanding Cosmic Law (the "will of the Gods") and living in accordance with it, rather than in opposition to it. At a mundane or practical level, the closest that academic scholars have ever come to understanding ancient mysticism is something they refer to as "sympathetic magic"—where the physical act of manipulating some symbol "here" has the ability to affect something "there."*

12. **"TO NOT OBSERVE THE RITES IS TO FALL."** *A unique formula drove the success of Mardukite Babylon, an understanding of cosmic wisdom and a tradition that was unparalleled in the ancient world. So long as the Temple District (priests and priestesses) and the Palace District (royal court) "observed the rites" of Mardukite Tradition, then*

happiness, prosperity and success were enjoyed by all. When usurpers or maligned rulers disregarded tradition, society greatly suffered. Often, the population revolted. The "Hand of Marduk" would touch upon some specific individual (even a foreigner) and bless them with visions and inspiration to ride into Babylon and replace the disgraced king, much to the welcome and celebration of the oppressed population. Then, the new king would prostrate themselves before the image of Marduk at his Temple, make appropriate offerings and vows, and give thanks for the privilege to lead the Babylonians.

13. UNDERWORLD RESURRECTION AND FUTURE LIVES.

Mardukite clergy held a unique understanding about spiritual life that distinguished them from others in the ancient world—and even other Mesopotamian traditions. All Mesopotamian traditions observed an immediate afterlife in the Underworld, but the Mardukites did not believe that one's spiritual existence permanently ended there. They believed in repeated incarnations in this material existence—and also that one could work their way upward "to be as like the Gods." Similarly to the Egyptians, the Mesopotamians believed that items buried with a body could assist them later; in this case, their journey to (and hopefully out of) the Underworld. Unlike the Egyptians, however, they did not believe that specific burial rites or posthumous incantations guaranteed someones Ascension—nor did they treat their kings as "living embodiments of a god" (as like pharaohs were viewed). Apart from Mardukite tradition, many Mesopotamians maintained more nihilistic beliefs influenced by older Sumerian "Gilgamesh" tablets—which suggested that "the Gods kept immortality for themselves and permit only death for humanity" so "eat and drink your fill" because one's destined Underworld is gloomy.

14. **ETHICS: "*GOOD*" AND "*BAD*."** *An enforceable moral law or "code" is present throughout ancient Mesopotamia, though the legal standards of King Hammurabi (nearly 4,000 years ago) are probably the most famous. Babylonian laws are rooted in a "utilitarian" philosophy (similar to the formula for #6 above), meaning they serve the "greatest good" for a healthy prosperous society as a whole by protecting the quality of life for all individuals concerned. A happy healthy society required a healthy fertile and properly maintained environment in which to exist. Wide-view ecological interests were synonymous with individual interests.*

15. **FAMILY RELATIONSHIP DETERMINES YOUR PLACE IN SOCIETY.** *An individual was*

born into a certain social class, but they were also capable of elevating their position thereafter. A citizen could own or inherit land, work in the family trade, become an educated professional, join the clergy, or even marry "up."

16. HUMANS BECAME AS THE RESULT OF A DIVINE ACT OF CREATION. *The specifics differ among Mesopotamian cultures, but all of the tablet records have one thing in common: they suggest that humans were created as a genetic result of "divine intervention" (as was the accelerated progress of their domestication/civilization). The oldest tablets indicate that a God was slain/sacrificed for their blood (genetics). The sixth tablet of the Mardukite Babylonian "Epic of Creation" describes the creation of humans (which is why the "Book of Genesis" indicates humans are made on the "sixth day") to serve the Gods, create and maintain temple-shrines—and the Mardukites are charged to keep watch and guard the "Gates."*

ACTIVITY

[Critical Thinking: It is important to question and analyze our beliefs, because they shape how we think, and ultimately what we do.]

1. Are any of these beliefs ones you hold

true?(yes/no)

2. Are there any that you don't agree with?
   #_____

3. List a belief/value you would add to the list.

   _____

   _____

Now, let's take a brief journey through the urban culture center of the once great city of Babylon. We'll quietly peer through the windows of the citizen's daily lives and note some details. Oh, to be a fly on a wall of this wondrous sprawling monument to a Golden Age of human civilization would be a priceless treasure for the collection of any museum.

SOCIAL CLASS, AGE & TITLES

The best historical example we have of Mesopotamian social class comes from the Law-Code of King Hammurabi (during the Old Babylonian era). A free-person or "citizen" might own land, if they were of the upper-class *awilum*; or they might not be landowners, and therefore be part of the work-a-day middle-class *mushkenum*.

Most scholarly translators reduce the lowest class, *wardum*, as "slave." This word did not carry the same meaning in Babylon that we find portrayed elsewhere. It literally meant that the individual did not own land and was not a free-person; therefore, not a true "citizen." This could include those in serious debt or working off criminal restitution, meaning that this social position was not necessarily permanent. By definition, most live-in "servants" of the Temple and Palace were also *wardum* (and treated well).

Unlike other "caste" systems in history, the social classes of Babylon are not fixedly mandated. These were simply economic observations, much as we might consider "class" today. These observations are based on an earlier pattern of settlement in southern Mesopotamia, which later became Babylonia. The earliest families settled on the best land and those that came later had to settle for less. Latecomers found themselves with no land at all. As a result, a systematic "stratification of wealth" simply occurred by the very nature of how early civilization progressively developed.

Women enjoyed more rights and equality in *Mardukite Babylon* than elsewhere in the ancient world, even compared to other Mesopotamian eras. This is often easy to distinguish based on periods and places where "Goddess" archetypes are given strong prominence. Positions in the Anunnaki pantheon are always presented as "Divine Couples"—a Goddess and God, both equally representative of whatever the aspect. Hence, for example, we find a highly venerated "moon god" and "sun goddess" alongside their respective spouses—which is culturally unique.

A strong "family unit" (household/home) was critical to societal success. Many of the marriage and inheritance laws of Hammurabi were intended to protect women. They could own their own property and even divorce husbands if mistreated. Babylonia also relied on *task specialization* for its success—individuals being productive in specific skilled activities.

Larger families (more children) were preferable in agricultural societies; they meant more help for working the farms (or other family businesses). No gender exclusions existed, but females generally excelled at managing household affairs; food preparation; textile-weaving; pottery-making; acting as mid-wives and physicians: creating music, poetry, jewelry and art; and of course, temple-priestesses.

IN BABYLONIAN
[FROM ROOT 'TO BE LITTLE']

SUḪÄRU	BOY
SUḪÄRTU	GIRL

ṢA/UḪURTU and BATÜSSU [ASSYR.]

WĂRTU or NU'ARTU are other words for "girl."

MUŠTENŬ means a "changed child" or post-pubescent adult, one who is old enough for marriage, which is celebrated as a special rite of passage—similar to the Jewish *bat-mitzvah* and the Latino *quinceanera*.

A young woman of fifteen, or BATŬLTU, has reached an age where she is permitted to marry. Sometimes marriages were even arranged by parents while the children were still young, but they would remain living at home until reaching maturity.

There was no literal word for "virgin," but *ki.sikil* meant a young maiden, who was assumed to be a virgin when she first married. *Sinnistštu* means an "adult woman"—though if unmarried, she might be referred to as a *nartu*. In Akkadian, "wife" is AŠŠATU or AŠTU; or ISSU in Assyrian. The life-cycle/age chart is given in the Sumerian language.

IN SUMERIAN		
AGE OVER 15 is ADULT		
SMALL GIRL	1 TO 5	MUNUS.TUR.TUR
GIRL	5 TO 10	TUR.MUNUS
OLDER GIRL	10 TO 15	MUNUS.TUR
WOMAN	15	MUNUS

40	LALŬTU is BLOOM OF LIFE
50	DAYS ARE SHORT
60	MET-LU-TU is MANHOOD
70	DAYS ARE LONG
80	ŠIBŬTU is OLD AGE
90	LITTŬTU is ADV. OLD AGE

SEASONS & MEASURING TIME

Ancient Babylonians observed two main seasons, essentially summer and winter. Traditional names for these seasons—*Enmeš* and *Enten* respectively—are derived from a Sumerian tale about two brothers (recorded on the "*Enmeš and Enten*" tablets). The spring equinox marked the start of the calender with the *Akiti* new year festival—the primary annual national holiday celebration, which lasted ten days. Later in the year, a transition between summer and winter was marked with a harvest festival.

The spring season also brought unpredictable challenges. The two main life-sustaining rivers often experienced furious flooding as the mountain snows melted. Water levels of the Euphrates River —BUR.AN.UN in Sumerian; *puratu* in Akkadian —often began rising in late-March or early-April;

whereas the Tigris River—I.DI.IK.LAT or *id-ig-na*—rose at the opposite time of year, and may have signaled the harvest (and a time for winter preparations).

Babylonians adopted, and continued advancing, the Sumerian's *sexagesimal* "base-60" system of mathematics for measuring space and time, including angles and coordinates. It is the basis of the 360-degree circle, the sixty-second minute and the sixty-minute hour. "60" has *12* whole number divisors: 1, 2, 3, 4, 5, 6, 10, 12, 15, 20, 30, and itself. The remarkably advanced level of Babylonian mathematics is still being deciphered in awe to this day.

The Anunnaki originally employed the *sexagesimal* numeric system and presumably taught it to the Sumerians. It is used to distinguish "hierarchical ranking" (roles or positions) in the Anunnaki pantheon. It was also key to mapping cartography of the "celestial sphere" that we recognize today as the "zodiac"—our perspective of a specific 360-degree ring that encircles the solar system and is divided into twelve 30-degree zones (or "houses"). This same structure evolved into our original calendars.

MONTHS

NISAN(U)—MARCH 21 (*Spring Equinox*)

AIARU [*ayaru*] — APRIL
SIMANU [*siwan*] — MAY
DU'UZU [*tammuz*] — JUNE
ABU [*ab*] — JULY
ALULU [*elul*] — AUGUST
TISHRITU [*tishri*] — SEPTEMBER 21
HESHWAN [*arahshamna*] — OCTOBER
KISLIMU [*kislev*] — NOVEMBER
TEBITU [*tebet*] — DECEMBER
SHEBATU [*sebat*] — JANUARY
ADDARU [*adar*] — FEBRUARY
[2nd *adar*] — (*aligns luni-solar year*)

CLOTHING

The need and desire to clothe one's body is perhaps the earliest distinction between "humans" and the "animal kingdom" here on Earth. Prehistoric signs of clothing exist beyond Mesopotamia. In fact, ancient "textiles" are most difficult to uncover directly with archaeology. Fortunately for us, there are surviving artistic depictions of Babylonian citizens, clergy and royalty, which have fared better over thousands of years than any physical remains of the clothing itself.

Early Sumerians are often depicted in leather and animal-skins, but the Babylonians greatly improved the textile industry. In addition to mastering agriculture for nourishment, farms often included domesticated sheep and goats (for their hair). The most common cloth type was *wool*, followed by *linen* for fancier fabrics. By the Neo-Babylonian era of Nebuchadnezzar II, the Assyrians had started importing *cotton* from Egypt.

Mesopotamians often used a large cloth to wrap about themselves as a main garment. There are also depictions of men wearing skirts (or kilts) and women wearing long gown-like tunics. Nobility and royalty are often shown wearing elaborately embroidered robes. Women were fond of fringes and tassels. One of the key differences in dress between men and women concerned the size of the cloth and direction of its wrap. Traditionally, female clothing crossed across the chest towards the left, or rational side of the brain; and a male crossed his across the chest towards the right, or intuitive side of the brain.

Typical accessories included things like brooches, shawls, decorated sandal-like shoes, bracelets, rings, necklaces, cylinder-seals, and amulets. Shoes were particularly important for priestesses and priests, since the act of touching the ground with the soles of one's feet was considered "unclean."

CHILDREN

Along the residential streets of Babylonia, it was quite common to see children at play. They had access to balls, musical instruments, played skip-rope and even developed a form of hockey. Not surprisingly, girls typically owned dolls, imagining themselves in the role of future mothers; boys, often idolizing the hunters and warriors, might play with small bow-and-arrow sets. Young ones also sought wooden and *terra-cotta* toy-miniatures of ships, chariots, wagons and animals—the same type of things a modern child would enjoy.

Most specialized trade learning occurred organically. The working class children usually stayed home to assist in the family business. The Sumerians established the oldest known educational institutions, but they began as subsidized private schools for the elite. These schoolhouses were often maintained in the Temple district (with the "*scribes*") and attendance with neither required, nor free. But, in Babylon, any social class or gender was permitted. Primary education focused on writing, followed by mathematics and history. Just as today, the purpose of learning was to be a more able, informed and productively successful citizen.

ANCESTORS & HOUSEHOLD GODS

Performing funerary rites and offerings for the dead was a key responsibility for the living. Offerings (*kispu*) of food (bread), drink (wine) and consecrated oils were made at the E.KISIGA ("House of Funerary Offerings") to prevent the spirit from "wander overseas and returning to haunt the upper world." At a small personal shrine devoted to the deceased love one, the simple ritual involves four main aspects:

1—PĀQIDU: the one who attends to (priest/ess)
2—KISPA KASĀPU: making the offering
3—MĚ RAQU: pouring water/libations; and
4—ŠUMA ZAKĀRU: the calling of the name.

These actions are performed exactly as written. 'One who attends to' is the arrival of the priest/ess. 'The act of making funerary offerings' is the literal cooking and/or acquisition of the offerings. The 'offerings' are left on the shrine-altar and the priest/ess waits outside for about thirty minutes. 'Pouring water/libations' is the act of pouring liquid offering for the spirit onto the ground outside. (You might have heard of this in other cultures, or the phrase "pour one out.") 'Calling of the name' is the final act of acknowledging and thanking the loved one (or ancestor).

The *Ilŭ rĕshi* (literally *"intermediary/middle gods"*) are one's "personal gods" (some academic

sources call them "household gods"). These are
the gods most common citizens prayed to (or petitioned) in their daily life. In some cases, they
might be the Anunnaki Gods of the traditional pantheon, but this wasn't a requirement. An *ashirtum*
("worship room") was a designated area of virtually every home. This personal shrine included an
offering table, set with votive statues and icons of
these personal gods.

The personal gods could either be represented by a
single statuette of a specific deity, or one statue
containing the seven angel-like figures representing the seven primary Anunnaki Gods. In many
ways, personal household reflects the rituals performed at the Temple pertaining to the "care and
feeding of family spirits (ancestors)."

The tools (aspects), actions and physical setup
tend to mirror the design and rituals of the Temple.
For example: after conducting the more formal funerary custom at the Temple-House, the care and
feeding of ancestor spirits continued similarly in
ones home—in an area designated specifically for
that. Similarly, the offerings an individual continues to make to one's "personal gods" (or Anunnaki
Gods) mirrors the more public ceremonies conducted by Temple priestesses and priests.

PROVERBS[*]

* A hostile act you shall not perform, that
fear of vengeance shall not consume you.

* You shall not do evil, that life eternal
you may obtain.

* Does a woman conceive when a virgin,
or grow great without eating?

* If I put anything down it is snatched
away; if I do more than is expected, who
will repay me?

* He has dug a well where no water is, he
has raised a husk without kernel.

* Does a marsh receive the price of its
reeds, or fields the price of their
vegetation?

* The strong live by their own wages; the
weak by the wages of their children.

* He is altogether good, but he is clothed
with darkness.

------

* Excerpt from: *Archeology and The Bible*, 3rd ed.,
Philadelphia: American Sunday School, 1920.

* The face of a toiling ox you shall not
strike with a goad.

* My knees go, my feet are unwearied;
but a fool has cut into my course.

* His ass I am; I am harnessed to a mule
—a wagon I draw, to seek reeds and
fodder I go forth.

* The life of day before yesterday has
departed today.

* If the husk is not right, the kernel is not
right, it will not produce seed.

* The tall grain thrives, but what do we
understand of it? The meager grain
thrives, but what do we understand of it?

* The city whose weapons are not strong
the enemy before its gates shall not be
thrust through.

* If you go and take the field of an enemy,
the enemy will come and take your field.

* Upon a glad heart oil is poured out of
which no one knows.

* Friendship is for the day of trouble,

posterity for the future.

*An ass in another city becomes its head.

* Writing is the mother of eloquence and the father of artists.

* Be gentle to your enemy as to an old oven.

* The gift of the king is the nobility of the exalted; the gift of the king is the favor of governors.

* Friendship in days of prosperity is servitude forever.

* There is strife where servants are, slander where anointers anoint.

* When you see the gain of the fear of god, exalt god and bless the king.

ACTIVITY

Armchair Academia: Compare the literal style and interpretive significance of these proverbs with the lines of "*Marduk's Tablet of Destiny*" given in the prefatory section titled "*Mardukite Zuism: A Brief Introduction.*"

ART

In ancient Mesopotamia, "art" was a new cultural innovation combining form and function, beauty and practicality. Urbanization permitted permanency and a greater ability to preserve one's property. This developed naturally into a basic desire for things to simply be "nicer." Artisans of every fashion were required for building up the Babylonian empire and everything within it.

From the glazed bricks that lined the processional streets and city-walls, to the very design of the Temples, Palaces, and every symbolic treasure kept inside them—each one contributed something unique to the publicly perceived power of the Babylonian tradition. Artisans and craftsmen were frequently commissioned by the Temple District to fashion various votive objects, ornate wall reliefs, special pottery, "seals," "stamps" and of course, religious statuary.

Due to its archeological longevity, Mesopotamian statues are perhaps the most famous demonstrations of artistic form and religio-political function. Naturally, we find large statues of Anunnaki Gods in the Temples. But others, like the immense human-headed winged-bull *lamassu*, were intended to stand as protective guardians at the entrance of Temples and libraries. In the Palace District, statues and grandiose wall-reliefs were created to venerate royalty and record historical events. Nearly all significant buildings had collections of small statues buried at the corners of its foundation.

There are other connections binding culture and religion in a way that cemented personal "faith" in the security of social systems and world order. A unique "glyptic" micro-sculpting art craft is found throughout the Ancient Near East and it plays an especially significant role in establishing the "legal" legitimacy of one's participation in society. It also required precision skill to carve the imagery on small "seals" and "stamps"—the smallest of which we've found are as tiny as one centimeter in diameter. But, here we find ancient origins of legally recognizable "signet rings" and "official marks."

Most official *cylinder seals* were 2-3 centimeters long (with a diameter usually half its length). They were made from a small piece of hard material—such as bone, shell, quartz, chalcedony, lapis lazuli, hematite, marble, agate and other precious stones. Their round cylindrical shape resembles a "bead"—some having holes running through to make it easier to carry or even wear them on a cord.

Intricate sunken or raised designs were carved with flint or copper tools, or a "bow-drill," to make the seal. Because it was used to make an impression in clay, any imagery and writing had to be reversed. Impressions were used to mark something "officially"—such as a personal signature on a contract, or a manufacturers mark—or for more decorative purposes. Imagery usually centered around Gods, their worshipers and other mythological symbolism and motifs. Personal seals might also serve as "amulets" and typically depicted specific deities, trees, animals, and prayers that an individual felt affinity for.

SCRIBES & SCHOOLHOUSES

"Who dwells in the place of scribal art,
like sun may they shine."

In ancient Mesopotamia, the word for "school" and "tablet-house" are synonymous: E.DUBBA in Sumerian; *bit-tuppi* in Akkadian. ['E' and '*bit*' (spoken '*bet*') both mean "house." The Sumerian root 'DUB' for "tablet" is treated as '*tup-*' in Babylon.] The purpose of the educational system was to develop young citizens into "scribes" (*tup-sharru*, "tablet-keeper"), meaning literate and "learned" members of society.

Prior to *Mardukite Babylon*, the educational system was private and exclusive to children (usually male, unless a daughter of royalty or future priestess) of elite families that could afford it. But, its public standardization during *Mardukite Babylonian* eras led to a greater and more productive society. Being able to *read* the tablets (rather than rely on someone else that could) added to the legitimacy of the structured civic systems represented on those tablets. Oral traditions are universal, but when a citizen could actually read their own contracts, or even the national laws and beliefs carved onto a eight-foot tall *stele* in the center of town, suddenly these "words that stay" took on greater significance.

Students required a strict intensive education if they aspired to walk the path of a *scribe*. They began attending school at tablet-houses around the age of ten (or earlier), then spent the next five years (until adulthood at 15) learning reading, writing, math and music, from sunrise to sunset, 24 days per month. [We don't know if school was held all year or not.] The average farmer, laborer or soldier did not necessarily possess these skills. Not all graduating students stayed on to develop even further learning as "scribes" (or physicians or clergy), but as civilization progressed, more of the serious professions required the ability to read and write.

Sumerian *cuneiform* was originally written using one's thumb nail. But around the Old Babylonian Era, a beautiful refinement of the script occurred for the Akkadian language with the invention of the *stylus* (*urbănu*) or scribe's-pen, cut from a reed plant. A Babylonian student studied both the Sumerian and national Akkadian languages. They retained many Sumerian words as a classical language, much like Europeans had treated Latin.

Archeologists are able to distinguish classroom sites from traditional library tablet-houses due to the sheer amount of tablets displaying "corrections." The teacher would write out tablets for a student to copy and then correct their assignments. Students also recited memorized lines. On a higher level, the standardization of public education in Babylon could also be considered the inception of systematized social learning or "indoctrination" of a worldview. Such things are so commonplace today that we seldom think of it—but in the ancient world, this innovation allowed for perpetual "domestication" (or civilizing) of an exponentially growing population (and in a region with a constant migrant influx).

Apart from schoolhouse tutoring and serving as clergy, the scribes were historians and lore-keepers responsible for the archival preservation, duplication and certification of critical literature and important documents. In *Mardukite Babylonia*, tablet-scribes developed a cult-like dedication to the Anunnaki scribe-god *Nabu*, inventor of the *stylus*. This "secret society" even maintained

Nabu's private temple-shrine, library and scribe-college in *Borsippa*, only ten miles away from *Babylon-city.* Where this present book has adopted a "temple-priestess perspective" of Mesopotamia, most other modern Mardukite Zuist literature (*by Joshua Free*) takes the "Borsippa scribe-priest of Nabu" approach to the Babylonian tradition.

MAY YOUR EXCEEDING WISDOM
GIVEN BY THE TABLETS OF NABU
NEVER CEASE ON THE CLAY
IN THE TABLET HOUSE.

IN THIS TABLET HOUSE
LIKE A SHRINE
FASHIONING EVERYTHING
MAY IT NEVER COME TO AN END.

TO THE JUNIOR SCRIBE
WHO PUTS HIS HAND TO THE CLAY
AND WRITES ON IT
MAY NABU THE ONE WHO SPEAKS
GIVE WISDOM.

MAY HE OPEN HIS HAND
IN THE PLACE OF WRITIING
MAY HE COME FORTH
LIKE THE SUN FOR THE SCRIBES.

THE STAR RELIGION

When the oldest astronomical observations were
recorded by the Sumerians, the Sun still entered
the celestial zone of *Taurus* on the vernal/spring
equinox (*March 21*), when the "new year" began.
The same constellation is still recognized as "the
Bull" today—originally in honor of *Enlil*, commander of the Anunnaki Gods during the
Sumerian era; what we still refer to as, the *Age of
Taurus* (*c.* 4130 BCE – 2160 BCE).

The Anunnaki Assembly (or Council) always intended this early "Sumerian" arrangement of the
pantheon as temporary, with *Marduk* awaiting his
era to command in the new *Age of Aries*. But 2160
BCE came and went and there was no peaceful
transition of power, nor even a recognition of a required forthcoming regime change. To add insult
to injury, Sumerian Kings reinvigorated public de-
votion in their old lunar-cults (dedicated to
Nanna/Sin) and *Inanna*/*Ishtar*-cults when establishing a new "Third Dynasty of UR" (UR III, *c.*
2120 BCE – 2000 BCE) in a last-ditch effort to
maintain control.

The UR-III attempt at a *Sumerian Renaissance* did
not completely thwart an eventual rise of *Mardukite Babylon*—but it required some ingenuity to
preserve Mesopotamian civilization in the wake of
a Sumerian cultural decline (*c.* 2150 BCE).

Babylon already existed as a proto-*Mardukite* settlement during UR-III, but it was never recognized as any kind of political center (or capital) during the Sumerian era. A period of chaotic confusion erupted among the population in the absence of a true authority and world order, leaving the region open to militant foreign invasions.

Toward the end of the *"Enlilite"* Sumerian era, the original *Mardukite* population (called *martu* or *amurru*; also *"Amorites"* in many academic texts) still primarily remained "outside" Mesopotamia. These nomadic *Nabu*-tribes awaited the *Age of Aries* in the desert wilderness to the west. Essentially, *"Martu"* is the same as saying *"Mardukite"* today; the population is named (using its own native language) for its chief Anunnaki-deity (*Marduk*).

With the "new age" dawning upon the land, the *Amorites* began a peaceful ethnic invasion, integrating themselves within the general Sumerian population. They shared the same Anunnaki pantheon. They even spoke a *semitic* language, similar to the Akkadians—*Akkadian* being the oldest *semitic* language. Their interests did not include killing, destroying, looting, and leaving Mesopotamia in ruin (the way other foreign invaders did), because this was to be their home and these were to be their people.

On a national (political) level, the *Amorite* cultural

invasion was met with strong resistance by the UR-III Dynasty. Even after that dynasty fell (2000 BCE), city-states such as *Larsa* and *Isin* continued to maintain their Sumerian independence (up until the reign of Hammurabi). It would take another hundred years for the *Amorites* to fully infiltrate Mesopotamia and establish the "First Dynasty of Babylon" *c.* 1900 BCE.

The *Mardukite Babylonian* empire thrived for three centuries before its capture by the Hittite military. Kassites from the east drove out the Hittites. They did their best to assimilate the Babylonian tradition, as did the later Assyrians, but after the fall of its First Dynasty (1595 BCE), it would take a millennium before an authentic *Mardukite Renaissance* occurred during the "Neo-Babylonian (Chaldean)" era (625 BCE – 539 BCE), which included Nebuchadnezzar II.

An *Anunnaki "Star Religion"* based on astronomical observation propelled Mesopotamian civilization from its start. But that esoteric information was of the Gods—and only served the priestesses and priests. The common person in society only understood the quality of their everyday life, and much of that was based on a strong faith in the Sumerian "systems" they participated. In order for Babylon to prosper in a post-Sumerian *Age of Aries*, the legitimacy for *Marduk*'s reign had to be established firmly in social consciousness.

Babylonians mythologically established *Marduk* as the new "*Bull of Heaven*"—calling him the "*Solar Calf*"—effectively replacing any position formerly held by *Enlil*. For example, in earlier literature, the Sun had been compared to an *ox*, or a farmer yoking his oxen to a shinning plow. A similar title was bestowed upon Marduk as he passed through the twelve zodiac house-signs: *Gudi-bir*, "the bull of light." When the Sun rose on the vernal/spring equinox, backed by one of the zodiac houses (zones), it was called the "directing bull"—"the bull who guides (the year)." Annual observation of a *Mardukite* version of the "New Year" festival in Babylon proved to be the key to perpetuating its religious success.

ANNUAL FESTIVALS

Astronomical and seasonal observation led to the original holidays of most ancient cultures. The "equinoxes" are the first significant dates that would have been recognized by the wise-ones that recorded natural and celestial data. They occur twice each year, in the spring and autumn, traditionally March 21 and September 21 (using modern standards). They are acknowledged on most ancient calendars and mark fundamental transitions in the annual cycle of life on Earth. Seasonal festivals also served an especially important function in agricultural societies and their continued survival.

In Mesopotamia, the spring equinox festival marked the start of the year on the first day of the month *Nisan(u)*. It was the single most important annual holiday. Its name—A.KI.TI in Sumerian; *Akitu* in Akkadian—meant "On Earth, Life," indicating seasonal renewal of the land and a time to begin planting barley. [In fact, an alternate (but less likely) translation of the Akkadian name could be "On Earth, Plant."] On a magical or symbolic level, the collective intention or social consciousness of a spring festival was directed to generate life and encourage abundance—ensuring fertility for the people, animals and natural environment.

As described in the previous section: on this first day of the year, the relative alignment between the Sun and the celestial sphere (or "zodiac"), as observed from Earth, also determined the current "*Age.*" This was important for *Mardukite Babylonians* to certify the national rituals and legitimize the position of Marduk. Revising earlier customs, the festival also celebrated the "divine marriage" of Marduk and Sarpanit—an earthling spouse, the daughter of an early Sumerian bloodline seeded directly by the Anunnaki. His selection of a "human" consort (elevated to goddess status in Babylon) only furthered the idea that Marduk sought to maintain a closer relationship with humanity than former Anunnaki Gods.

On a local political level, the annual *Akiti Rituals* cemented "Divine Right" of the king to rule as a representative intermediary between the general population and cosmic order. But, of course, the clergy were responsible for conducting the rites, which included the king temporarily surrendering their royal regalia and kingship to Marduk (or a statue thereof). Priestesses and priests ultimately determined whether or not a king's right-to-rule would be returned to him for another year—presumably based on how well he had ruled the previous year (and perhaps whether or not it aligned with the will of the Temple District). Although mainly symbolic drama, the very fact of its inclusion in a public liturgy is why *anti-Mardukite* and tyrannical usurper kings did not "observe the rites."

Above all, the "New Year" *Akiti-Akitu* festival was a celebration and commemoration of the *Mardukite* pantheon—*Marduk* and *Sarpanit*, and, of course, *Nabu* (his adopted heir apparent) and *Teshmet* (*Tasmit*). A ten-mile procession from *Borsippa* carried the official statue of *Nabu* to attend the festival in *Babylon-city* and participate in the rites. There was also a dramatic reenactment of the *Babylonian "Epic of Creation,"* displaying Marduk conquering the forces of the Universe (or *Tiamat*, the Cosmic Dragon). The entire festival period lasted twelve days.

From the available cuneiform tablet records recovered and deciphered, we know that a "harvest festival" also occurred each year at the autumn equinox (the first day of the month of *Tashritu*). Early scholars blurred any details about the autumn-harvest festival with the spring festival (or even earlier Sumerian beliefs) that academicians confusingly reference both *Babylonian* festivals as *Akiti*. This is in part because of UR-III tablet interpretations that may refer to an "*A-ki-ti* of seed time" (spring) and an "*A-ki-ti* of barley-cutting" (autumn).

Mardukite Babylonians reserved the "dark half" of the year to acknowledge the "other side" of the pantheon—mainly *Inanna-Ishtar* and *Dumuzi* (*Tammuz*). The symbolic ritual motif for autumn and winter undoubtedly turned toward "death"— hence we find a ceremonial reenactment of "*Inanna's Descent to the Underworld*" and emphasis on other mythological themes concerning her lover, a slain god-king renewed. And to differentiate this autumn festival (from the spring) for an authentic new modern *Mardukite* standard, we have adopted the name "*Zagmuk*" from an archaic Sumerian word for the same.

Additional records refer to other publicly observed "community fire festivals" where consecrated symbols representing the wickedness and iniquities of society would be burned in effigy. Such details are included in a companion volume —"*The Maqlu Ritual Book*" or "*Anunnaki Rites: New Standard Zuist Edition.*" Whether or not these were assigned to the "solstices" or some other specific dates, we cannot be absolutely certain. In the *Mardukite* tradition of modern "Mesopotamian Neopaganism," it has become a custom to observe the *Maqlu* ritual on the eve of October 31, paralleling the Celtic *Samhain*.

"Let us learn to appreciate there will
be times when the trees will be bare,
and look forward to the time
when we may pick the fruit."
-ANTON CHEKHOV-

⚜ 2 ⚜
BABYLONIAN GODS & GODDESSES

"Through Marduk, the power of Eridu—incantation-prayer and 'intention'—was taught to the scribes of Nabu and the Mardukite Priests, who were taught to attract and compel the 'gods' in the name of Marduk, always incanting the word-formula of the highest order: Nabu invoked by way of the name of Marduk; Marduk invoked by way of the name of Enki, Our Father, who in turn would invoke by the name of Anu—and so was born the concept of magical hierarchies, an ideal that was convoluted and obscured when employed later, such as during the Middle Ages and particularly distorted by the Judeo-Christian paradigm as evident in many popular grimoires"
—Joshua Free, Tablet-W, Book of Marduk

BABYLONIAN RELIGION

The Anunnaki pantheon dominated the social and religious consciousness of Mesopotamia for 6,000 years, right up until the arrival of Arabs and Islam. When the Akkadian language and Babylonian tradition replaced the former Sumerian culture, it retained the same Anunnaki pantheon. The names were changed to match the new language; and hierarchical positions were updated to be consistent with the new *Mardukite* emphasis propagated by the capital city of Babylon—in honor of its patron god, Marduk, and in recognition of the "*Age of Aries.*"

The rich culture, advanced knowledge and spiritual tradition of Babylon inspired envy and awe by those living in the surrounding areas. While the Sumerians and Babylonians observed what we consider the "original" Anunnaki tradition, that tradition and its lore did not remain exclusive to Mesopotamians. It spread to those cultures emerging along its perimeter and evolved further from there. The *Arameans, Canaanites, Cimmerians, Edomites, Elamites, Gutians, Hittites* and *Hurrians*, all assimilated their own diluted interpretations of Babylonian Anunnaki tradition in their own language, for their own religious purposes and cultural flavors. The *Assyrians* were the most famous example of this —modeling their chief god *Ashur* directly from Marduk. The Assyrian King *Ashurbanipal* was also quite adamant about owning a copy of every piece of significant tablet literature from Babylon for his personal library.

Ancient Mesopotamians shared a unique relationship with the Anunnaki Gods. For a time, they resided on Earth in Sumerio-Babylonian city-states, or at least visited the region frequently. They kept themselves separate from the people—residing in homes elevated high above the general population. There is also evidence to suggest that they "appeared" to other ancient cultures on the planet as well, since we find a consistent pattern represented in many "mythologies."

While some ambiguous recollections are certainly retained in Judeo-Christian *Old Testament* scriptures, most later cultures influenced by this Ancient Near Eastern experience—such as the Greeks and Romans—did not have the same direct contact with their version of the deities. For most ancient religions, the gods are "distant" yet watchful. And while classical-era statues and legends depicted anthropomorphic "humanoid" pantheons, the actual physical presence of a deity is always considered "elsewhere"—often some remote area or inaccessible mountain peak.

The idea of a visible, yet unapproachable, home for gods began in the Ancient Near East. Although mountains can be viewed in the far-off distance, the landscape of Mesopotamia is quite flat. One of the Anunnaki founded each of the original city-states and became its "patron-god." Various temple-shrines, like churches, dedicated to a specific "patron-god" (and their other "family members") were built in the Temple District and elsewhere throughout the city. These were places where citizens could interact with the priestesses and priests serving as intermediaries to the gods, but they were not the actual residence of the deity. Construction of that residence was reserved for the tops of large ominous artificial mountains—called *ziggurats*—constructed from clay bricks and off-limits to the general population (lay persons or non-clergy).

Babylonian priest-astronomers named the seven ancient planets the "wandering gods of the fixed zones"—and in agricultural terms, the seven "bellwethers" (named for the head bell-wearing cattle leading a herd). Note that in the ancient system, the Sun and the Moon are treated as planets. There is some evidence to suggest that Sumerio-Babylonian clergy were aware of Neptune, Uranus and Pluto—but since they were not visible to the naked eye they were considered too distant to directly influence affairs on Earth, when they could more easily employ "closer" intermediaries (lesser gods). Where the Sumerian religion adopted a twelvefold hierarchy (mirroring arrangements of the original Anunnaki Assembly and the "zodiacal wheel"), the system adopted in *Mardukite Babylon* is sevenfold, with a direct relationship with the planets, days of the week, colors, notes of music, and so forth.

The Babylonian pantheon spiritually aligned

Anunnaki roles with the visible planets—but they did not primitively confuse the persona of the deity with the actual planet (in the way most archaeologists interpret). Contrary to popular beliefs supported by contemporary historians: the "star god mythology" at the foundation of Babylonian religion was not a primitive attempt to understand natural forces. Even if that were the case elsewhere, the type of animistic shamanic characteristics found in those cultures are not present in the "urban religion" of Babylon. Although the clergy acknowledged a *Divine Spark* present in all life, they did not believe, for example, that a *"storm-god"* was literally present *in* the wind. When a deity name on a tablet referred to a planet, it was preceded by the MUL.MUL sign (meaning "star-star" or "twin star"); when the personage of a god is indicated, the AN or *ilu* sign precedes it.

THE ANUNNAKI GODS

The Babylonian *"Mardukite"* perspective explored here is different than the original Sumerian pantheon inspired by the Anunnaki "elder tradition." It is dedicated to the "younger pantheon," the offspring of Enlil and Enki (both sons of Anu). The "elders" are still acknowledged in Babylonia during the *Age of Aries*, but their they move on to become more distant historical figures and their hierarchical positions become filled by the "younger" group. Everyone gets a promotion.

In the Babylonian pantheon, the Sumerian "elders"—Anu, Enlil and Enki—form a "Supernal Trinity" that is outside of (or above) the sevenfold "planetary gate" system. Unlike other traditions, the "significant other" or "consort" (husband, wife...) of a god was equally "worshiped" alongside their respective partners. This is why the similarly named singular planets are referred to as "twin stars." The "elder" divine couples are then: Anu and Antu; Enlil and Ninlil; and Enki and Ninki. Their "younger" offspring are represented in the *Mardukite* tradition as follows:

> NINURTA/NINIB (Saturn energy current)
> MARDUK (Jupiter energy current)
> NERGAL (Mars energy current)
> SHAMMASH/UTU (Solar energy current)
> ISHTAR/INANNA (Venus energy current)
> NABU (Mercury energy current)
> NANNA/SIN (Lunar energy current)

However, we again must recognize that these positions are shared with a consort: Ninurta and Bau; Marduk and Sarpanit; Nergal and Ereshkigal; Ishtar (Inanna) and Dumuzi; Nabu and Teshmet; Shammash (Utu) and Aya; and Nanna (Sin) and Ningal.

These same "powers" and "forces" have historically appeared to humans all over the earth. Mankind followed, and fell in with the plan of "deifying" these beings into "gods" complete with religious traditions and beliefs defended by the sword. At first, offerings presented by the public to the temples were literally to feed the Anunnaki themselves. But once the Gods "left" Earth, the offering would continue on to feed the clergy and their families, perpetually increasing the security and wealth of the Temple District—even when distributing it among the "poor." Eventually the shrines and temples were left emptied, seemingly forgotten by humanity as they, themselves, eventually felt empty and forgotten.

CARE AND FEEDING OF THE GODS

If the past fifteen years of modern *Mardukite* literature has established one definitive point, it is that the concept of "magic" is synonymous with (practically indistinguishable from) "religion" in Mesopotamia. Whether a member of the clergy or a lay-citizen, the whole spiritual system in Babylon emphasized one's personal relationship with the Anunnaki Gods (and what they represented). Essentially, we are talking about the original system of "religious temple magic." It does not require the same intricacy and complexity found in later forms of "kabbalistic magic" (the basis of modern "magick") that became popular during the

Middle Ages (and which were actually mutated evolutions of Mesopotamian magic).

To further illustrate just how "basic" such *religious magic* is, it is interesting to note that since the 2009 release of *The Complete Anunnaki Bible*, the suggested "ceremonial formula" for modern *Mardukites* can be reduced to a single paragraph, summarized on the Tablet-B Series:

> The priest(ess) is always to observe the pious ways, and the *Rites of Offering* at the *Altars of the Gods*. This is traditionally performed by singing praise ("hymns") and intoning "prayers" (requests) recorded on the tablets while making offerings of incense, grain and libations of water, honey and buttermilk (and in some cases, wine); and in some cases stones such as alabaster, gold, and *lapis-lazuli*. Sacred, "blessed" or "holy" oil frequently appears in ancient Babylonian rites, and may have even possessed psychotropic properties, though the exact mixture has been lost—save for one formula which requires the mixture of gold flakes [a stone] with the essences of *"binu"* [a shrub/tree] and *"mastakal"* [an herb]. The offerings were traditionally

placed in bowls before icons, images or idols of the deity in the temples.

While the passage serves as an adequate introduction to the subject, we will be providing more details in this present book for those desiring to make a modern practice of this. A modern practitioner may not have access to ancient Babylonian temples, but the tradition was also observed as a "personal religion" by the citizens in their everyday lives. The activities observed at the Temple were duplicated on a personal level in one's own home. The typical religious devotee maintained a special room or area that adequately served one's purposes. Such symbolic personal practices were common even when an individual made their "standard" offerings at the Temple.

"*The Pious Ways,*" by Babylonian standards, followed the cliché adage that "cleanliness is next to godliness." No true "divine offering" could be made before first clearing and blessing a space, sleeping in said space, cleansing one's self, wearing clean linens, anointing with oils, and finally, removing one's shoes. Any "intentions" are stated (directed or prayed to the deity) during the act of making the offering. Whether approaching the tradition as a clergy-member (accepting and making offerings) working at the Temple, or a citizen practicing in their own home, the basic steps are the same.

Physical components appearing in one's own personal shrine (or prayer room) generally imitated what is found at the Temple, including (but not limited to): an altar, an altar cloth, a statue (idol) or other deity symbol, a censer for incense, and at least one lamp, candle (or tealight). Each of the Temples were dedicated to a specific *divine aspect*, but *Babylon-city* included a separate Temple-shrine for each of the *Seven* (among others).

To provide an example of a basic setup, we present the elements found on the author's own priestess altar—which is a *Teshmet*-dedicated shrine. The altar itself is made of wood, with a copper symbol inlaid on the top; an incense wand (of *myrrh*) rests on a stand (or burner) on the left; a crystal clear goblet of pomegranate wine; a statuette of the intended deities; a bundle of raw wheat; a bronze offering plate for dates, fish, and fine white-flour bread with butter on top; a bowl of honey for the bread; and a candle attached with gum to a small copper plate (to catch the wax).

An individual did not have to choose one particular Anunnaki God in exclusion to the others—although one generally dedicated a single *Rite of Offering* to just one aspect. Also remember that "divine couples" were worshiped together as a single aspect. So, it was not uncommon to find representative images of both the Goddess and the God at the same altar (or shrine). Responses to one's "prayers" and adoration could be interpreted in a variety of ways, such as: contact through dream communication, "*gnosis*" (spontaneous revelation), sense of a divine presence, and/or a physical manifestation of synchronicity (that some might mistake as mere coincidence).

Raw ingredients offered at the Temple were not hand delivered up to the god of the *ziggurat* "as is." It was the responsibility of certain clergy to prepare a meal—or a *tākultu*—which included:

NAQŬ – drink/libation (water, beer, wine).
NINDABŬ – grain (bread, barley).
NISANNU – fruit (dates).
NIQŬ – meats, poultry, fish.

Other nonperishable gifts were also graciously accepted by all the deities—so it was common to see such things being carried to the Temple as offerings. These might include: baskets; colored linen and wool garments; cedar and cypress wood (or items); purple-violet and royal-blue goods; precious metals (silver, bronze, iron and gold); and precious stones, such as *ud* (ash), *lapis lazuli*, *ka* (basalt), *muhu-digili* and *mushgarru* stones.

* * * * * * *

This chapter goes on to include a basic ritual formula for making offerings, and then a basic description for the primary Anunnaki Goddesses

and Gods of the Babylonian pantheon (and spiritual literature of the *Mardukite* period) and their
residences. This information supplements data giv-
en in another volume available for this series:
"*Sumerian Religion*" by Joshua Free, simultaneously released as "*Anunnaki Gods: New Standard
Zuist Edition.*"

> To truly understand ancient Mesopotamian
> religion, one thing must be stressed above all
> else: this tradition was founded when the
> Anunnaki Gods were present, residing on, or
> openly visiting, the planet. They were not yet
> all distant memories. They certainly were not
> primitive anthropomorphic illusions used to
> understand natural forces. They were not yet
> restricted to communicating in visions and
> dreams—or burning hedges. For this reason
> (and many others described in this book),
> Mesopotamian religion uniquely stands apart
> from any others in the ancient world.

In physical forms, occupying biological avatars
(regardless of their nature otherwise), the Anunnaki Gods were, in many ways, just like us. They
required sustenance and therefore preferred food
and drink that was pleasurable to consume. They
enjoyed music and dancing. They traveled to various cities for festivals, holidays and commemora-
tions. They required beds to sleep in and enjoyed
the pleasures of marital (and at times extramarital)

intercourse. They had to wash, dress, and even preferred to wear the pleasant odors of perfumes.

FORMULA FOR MAKING OFFERINGS

1. LIGHT THE INCENSE
(*smoke carries speech to the divine*)

2. LIGHT THE LAMP/CANDLE
(*aesthetics, atmosphere and light*)

3. GREET DEITY/STATUETTE/SYMBOL
(*address/acknowledge deity*)

4. WELCOME THEM TO YOUR SPACE

5. OFFER THE MEAL

6. OTHER OFFERINGS/GIFTS
(*any special items*)

7. EXPLAIN OFFERINGS
(*their intended use*)

8. PLACE ON ALTAR
(*leave for ten to thirty minutes and when appropriate edibles are consumed, liquids poured into earth*)

9. THANK DEITY AND WELCOME THEM TO RETURN AGAIN

TESHMET
Tashmit / Teshmetu / Tasmitu

"While Nabu spoke, Teshmetu listened."

Sometimes called "The Great Goddess" and "Bride of E.SAGILA," she is the wife of Nabu (who is the God of wisdom, writing and learning, representative of the planet Mercury). Her name is derived from the Akkadian *šamû*, which means "the granting (of requests)." Like her husband, she is equally famous for her wisdom—known as a merciful mediator, a protector from evil, and a goddess of love and potency.

Dwelling in the E.KUA or E.ZIDA at *Borsippa* (the cult center of Nabu's clergical scribes), Teshmet is considered benevolent and merciful, interceding with her divine powers on behalf of the people. She is the "One Who Listens" and epitome of what it means to be a "twin star" to her consort. She is the "listener" to his "speaker"— and the "Lady of Hearing and Favor," called upon to act as an intermediary to Nabu (on behalf of those in need). Dedicating a shrine of mulberry and SIDARŪ-wood, with a golden footstool, would be a most acceptable gift for the "Lady of Listening." Her astronomical sign is Capricorn.

According to tablet records, Teshmet is the daughter of Uraš (Urash), the archaic Sumerian name of

Enlil's mother (and mother to Ninsun or Bau). Even independent of Nabu, she was the patron goddess of Dilbat, with a cult center also at Kalhu-city. In the Sumerian language she is sometimes referred to as Nana; and in Assyria she is called Nisaba (which archaeological scholars have commonly mistaken for a "female Nabu"). The transliterated name used most commonly in our *Mardukite* literature is as it appears in Old Babylon (Akkadian): Tashmetum.

SARPANIT
Sarpanitu / Zarpanit / Zirbanitu / Erua

In the *Mardukite* Babylonian pantheon, "Queen Zērbānītu" is the "Queen of Totality; of the Whole Universe (All Creation)." As the "twin-star" to Marduk (the "new" Jupiter, replacing Enlil), her husband, she was elevated high in the pantheon as the patron goddess of Babylon; Erua or Belitu —"one who creates the seed," the "lady of ladies" and "beloved spouse"; and, perhaps most literally, the "shinning one from Zarpa."

Sarpanit is represented as the archetypal "mother goddess" in Babylon, the "giver of progeny" often depicted pregnant (as Erua)—supposedly with the Marduk's heir-son, Nabu. *E.dara'anna* is the name of her room-cell within E.SAGILA at *Babylon-city*. As a "creator goddess" she is considered a protector of the country (*Babylonia*). Similar to how Teshmet acted as an intermediary for Nabu, Sarpanit was known as an "interceder of the faithful," often petitioning Marduk on behalf of the people. Her symbol is the rising moon.

ISHTAR (VENUS)
Inanna / Astarte / Ashtoreth / Mylitta

Perhaps the most famous Goddess in the history of Earth, with an ambitious reach that spread from Sumer to virtually every ancient culture—Inanna or Ishtar—the Goddess of Ten-Thousand Names. She is the "exalted lady" and "valiant queen of the gods." She is the "ruler of heaven and earth" and "star of lamentation"; the "lady of battles," the "courtesan of the gods," the "arbitress," and "she who discloses pitfalls (or snares)." She is the "hierodule of heaven" (*Annunitum*) represented by, and sharing a name with, the planet Venus—and her Anunnaki numeric rank is "15."

Starting from the earliest Sumerian era, Inanna is the goddess of sex and war, of gentle rains and thunderstorms, Lady of the evening, and the morning star. She is the *Enlilite* "everymans" goddess— prayed to by men when in battle and when in bed; daughter of Nanna (Sin), the Moon God; brother to Shammash, the Sun God; and sister of Ereshkigal, the Underworld Goddess. She originally is betrothed to Marduk (in an effort to unite the *Enlilite* and *Enki'ite*/*Mardukite* Anunnaki lineages for the *Age of Aries*), but as both of them ambitiously sought to "*be on top,*" that union never occurred. She is still given the position of Venus in the Babylonian pantheon, but *not* as the "Lady of Babylon" (consort of Marduk).

Evidence of her cult-like worship is found in all Sumerian (*pre-Mardukite*) traditions. Young, beautiful, and impulsive, Inanna is given an exceptional degree of prominence in Sumer for being part of the "younger generation" of Anunnaki. She is called *Annunitum* or "Anu's Beloved"—especially favored by Anu, her grandfather, who gave her the E.ANNA Temple in Uruk to establish her cult center. Of course, she also had many other shrines throughout Mesopotamia, including the E.TURKALAMMA in Babylon (where her Akkadian name is "Ishtar"). Her symbols include the cow, doves, and (as it appears on the walls of *Babylon-city*) lions.

ERESHKIGAL (AND NERGAL)
Allatu / Leluwani / Allani (and Erra)

Ereshkigal is "Queen of the Netherworld" and "Lady of the Great Place (Deep Earth)—the Goddess of Irkallu (*the Underworld*). As a daughter of Nanna (Sin), she is sister to Inanna (Ishtar) and

Shamash (Shammash). Her "divine consort" is the "god of light"—Nergal (represented by the planet Mars). Their daughter was made famous in the "Descent" tablet cycles, the "Black Goddess" and "Goddess of Death"—Namtar (who is sometimes called in exorcism rites to liberate a sick individual presumed to be possessed by spirits.

The other "attendants" of the Underworld and Death served Ereshkigal and operated in specialized groups. The *gallû* were "constables"; the *rabisu*, "deputies"; and the *umu* were "day-demons." Ereshkigal's primary job was to guard the Gates of the Underworld ("Death"/"between-lives" area) and the Fountain-of-Life. Ereshkigal and Nergal shared a cult-center and Temple in the city of Kutha. To the *Mardukite* Babylonians, Nergal was also known as Erra, the "God of Destruction and Pestilence" or Salbatanu, "He Who Keeps Plague Constant"—and his Anunnaki numeric rank was "8."

Gender-roles of the Sumerian Underworld "divine courtship drama" are the opposite of what we find in the Greek recension (of Hades and Persephone) that a reader may be more familiar with. It is the origin of later agricultural traditions where the seasonal/astronomical cycles are aligned with stories to establish a "mythology." The cuneiform tablet-cycle titled "*Ereshkigal and Nergal*" describes the Goddess at first residing alone and sexually frustrated in her dark and desolate otherworld kingdom. She eventually compels the "god of light" (Nergal) to spend the "dark half" of the year in the Underworld as her sexual partner.

BAU (AND NINURTA / SATURN)
Ninegal / Nungal / Gula / Ninisina / Ugallu / Ninunuga
(and Ningirsu / Pabilsag)

Starting in the Third Millennium BCE, Bau is called Ninisina the "Lady of Isin"—patron-goddess of *Isin-city* and its dynasty—along with her "divine spouse," Ninurta (representative of the planet Saturn). A daughter of Anu and Nammu (Enki's sister), and sister to Nanna, she is of the mid-generation Anunnaki that ranked high in the Sumerian pantheon. In fact, Ninurta is Enlil's heir-son, the pre-Babylonian "Marduk" figure of the *Enlilites.* Their cult-center remained in Isin during the *Mardukite* era, where she was named Gula in the new Akkadian language.

In prayers and rituals, Bau is petitioned as the Goddess of Healing and as a "guardians spirit." She is the "Lady Who Brings the Dead Back to Life." Her religious icons and statues commonly display her seated next to a dog. The act of a dog licking wounds was considered a symbol of healing. In these artistic depictions, her dog is her personal guardian, named *Tuni-iu-sag*. In the Sumerian tradition (as observed in Isin), the son *Damu,* and daughter *Gunura* or *Ninazu,* of Nin-isina and Pabilsag are also physicians and healers of renown.

AYA (AND SHAMMASH / SUN)
Sherida (and Utu / Uttu / Uddu)

In Babylo-Akkadian, the cuneiform name *ilu-Šamaš* is transliterated as Shamash or Shammash (Š = "*sh*"). The name *Šamaš* or *Samas* is the same for the Anunnaki God as for the actual Sun-star (though the two could be distinguished either by context or prefixing the word with a "MUL" sign). However, his consort, Aya (or Sherida in the old Sumerian language) is named specifically for the Sun at "dawn"—making her the first individual in recorded history to be named "Dawn" in a native language. In this wise, Mesopotamian tradition is particularly unique for the fact that it acknow-ledges a prominent "Solar Goddess" to represent feminine aspects of the Sun.

The sun represents the brilliance and radiant en-ergy experienced by lifeforms on Earth—its light allowing the organic life to grow, and by solar cycles we often measure its lifespan. The fiery nature of the Sun-star (and its deities) is frequently called upon during incantations to "incinerate iniquities" and "illuminate truth." Even in *Mardukite* tradition, it is Shammash and the Sun that is representative of legal justice and ethics. The graphic at the top of the *stele* displaying Hammurabi's famous law in Babylon actually depicts the legal code resulting from an encounter with Shammash, not Marduk.

The Anunnaki numeric rank given to the Sun is "20." Unlike the elder god-couples appearing in the Sumerian pantheon—Anu-60/Antu-55 (Heaven and Uranus), Enlil-50/Ninlil-45 (Air-Space and Jupiter), Enki-40/Ninki-35 (Earth and Neptune) and Nanna-30/Ningal-25 (the Moon)—the positions for "divine couples" representing the Sun-20, Venus-15, Mercury-12 and Saturn-8, apparently share sacred numeric values. Therefore, we might presume that the number "20" applies equally to both Aya and Shammash.

NINGAL (AND NANNA-SIN / MOON)
Nikkal (and Nanna / Su-en / En-zu)

Ningal—"the great lady"—is the original Sumerian female lunar archetype (the Moon Goddess, a daughter of Enki, Mother to Inanna-Ishtar and Shammash). She was worshiped alongside her divine husband, Nanna (the Moon God, firstborn son of Enlil and Ninlil, Father of Inanna-Ishtar and Shammash), at their city cult-centers in Ur and

Harran. In Ur, their temple—E.GISH-SHIR-GAL
—translates to mean "House of the Great Light."
One might note that in this old Sumerian cosmolo-
gical lore, the "divine couple" representing the
"Moon" is responsible for birthing "Venus" and
the "Sun."

Nanna and Ningal are particularly significant deities in the predominantly "lunar" or "dark"
Sumerian tradition that predates the Babylonian
era—yet they remain in the *Mardukite* system.
where Nanna (the Moon) is named Suen or Sin in
Akkadian. But these various names do not generic-
ally all mean "moon." The full name/word *nannar*
indicates "light of the full moon." Another archaic
one, AS-IM-BABBAR, is the "light of the new
moon." And *su-en* is specifically the "light of the
crescent moon."

In Anunnaki numerology, Nanna's rank or value is
"30"—the number of days in a month, based on
the number of degrees designating one-twelfth of a
360-degree circle. There are some archaic writings
that suggest the Moon was intentionally placed in
its ancient position (which was much closer than it
is today) in order to regulate the months. Ningal's
number is "25."

NINKI (AND ENKI)
Damkina / Damgalnuna
(and EA / Nudimmud)

Ninki (or Damkina) is called "Mistress of the In-cantation of the Deep," a reference to the "Incantation of the Deep" or else the "Incantation of Eridu"—the first "magical incantation" de-veloped in prehistory and recorded on archaic tablets. Her name indicates she is "Lady of the Earth" or "Lady of Earth (Life)," and as such, she is named the consort of Enki, "Lord of the Earth." He is also named Ea (E.A.), the words for "home" and "water"—yet another reference to the pro-to-Sumerian Anunnaki legacy of *Eridu-city*.

Enki and Ninki governed the power inherent in the spoken word, which is to say the "magic spell" or "incantation." Their domain and cult-center at the "Temple of the Deep" (or "Temple of the Abyss") in *Eridu* earned a reputation as the "City of Magic and Sorcery"—the original "ancient mystery school" of the sciences, magic, technology—and knowledge of the "Arts (Systems) of Civilization," referred to on archaic tablets in plural as the Di-vine *ME*, pronounced "*may.*"

Enki is the eldest son of Anu and half-brother of Enlil (by a different mother). Collectively, these three deities (and their divine counterparts) com-prise the original proto-Sumerian Anunnaki religious pantheon on Earth, of which is later treated as the "Supernal Trinity" of the spiritual system. Enki maintains his numeric value of "40" in both Sumerian and Babylonian tradition—and "35" for Ninki.

In Babylon, Ninki is a significant "Mother Goddess"—she is recognized as Marduk's mother. Marduk was raised in Eridu as Enki's heir-apparent, learning the arts of magic and science and the "systemology" of existence. Enki is the original "God of Wisdom and Magic" during the *Age of Taurus*—although as his apprentice, by the *Age of Aries* it is Marduk that is treated as "Master of Magicians."

MARDUK (JUPITER)
Amar-utu / Asar-luhi / Bel / Merodach / Sanda

By definition, Marduk is the central deity of the *Mardukite* tradition and patron-god of Babylonia. His cult-center and temple, the E.SAG-ILA, was located in *Babylon-city.* The heir-son and apprentice of Enki. in proto-Sumerian Eridu, he was named *Asar-luhi*, and even *Amar-utu*, the "Solar-Calf"—as he was intended to inherit *"Enlilship"* during the *Age of Aries.* His consort, Sarpanit, was equally elevated in the new Babylonian Anunnaki pantheon as a high status Goddess (and is discussed elsewhere in this volume).

As Mesopotamia entered the *Age of Aries*, its population experienced a Babylonian reformation of the prior Sumerian systems. The Akkadian language and refined cuneiform script became a national standard, even among diplomatic correspondence with other foreign nations of the Ancient Near East, including Egpyt. The "Divine Right" of Marduk to lead the pantheon and become the "Lord of Lords" is spiritually solidified and politically cemented in social consciousness with the document (tablet series) called the *Enuma Elis* or "*Babylonian Epic of Creation.*" In that document, Marduk becomes "Lord of the Fifty Names" assuming the powers and personas of all the deities —and upgraded from the Anunnaki numeric rank of "10" to "50" (as previously held by Enlil in the Sumerian pantheon).

Ancient and classical cultures emerging after *c.* 2000 BCE were all highly influenced by the *Mardukite Babylonian* tradition—most of which assimilated a version of Marduk to be at the head of their pantheons, of course, adapting the lore to their own language and flavors. Its unique style of "monaltry" is the closest thing to "monotheism" described in ancient writings. In this case, other deities exist, but are treated as emissaries or ambassadors for a supreme deity, who is really the sum of the others by themself.

For example, another epitaph for Marduk is Bel, which is meant to signify "Lord" (with a capital "L"). In the nearby *Western Semitic* tradition emerging in Canaan *c.* 1500 BCE, Marduk becomes "*Ba'al*" or "*Baal.*" In addition to the *bow*, one of the primary symbols and weapons of Marduk is called the *imhullu*, and it resembles a long three-prong fork-like trident that allegedly produced lightning. Combing this with the astronomical association of the planet Jupiter and the Greeks then had an archetype for "*Zeus.*" Closer to home, in another example, the Assyrians—who highly revered the cultural superiority of Babylon and even held an occupation of the dynasty for a time—modeled their own chief-god "*Ashur*" after Marduk.

NABU (MERCURY)
Muduggasa / Tutu (Thoth) / Nebo / Apollo

"As the writer or scribe of the gods, he records their decisions. As proclaimer or herald of the gods, he announces them. Trust in the words of Nabu; trust in no other god."

Apart from his father, Marduk, the god Nabu is perhaps the second most significant deity in *Mardukite Babylonian* tradition. His clerical scribe-cult and temple-home was located at *Borsippa*—

which was practically a suburb of Babylon, located a mere dozen miles from its city center. He first emerges in religio-political history as a messianic-prophet proclaiming the coming of the *Mardukite* tradition for his father's new *Age of Aries.* His wife, Teshmet or Tasmitu, was the divine "listener" complimenting his role as "speaker" (and she is discussed elsewhere in this volume).

In Babylonian tradition, Nabu is both the embodiment of wisdom and an agricultural nature-god— with "12" being his sacred number (numerologically aligning him with the measure of Space and Time). In many ways he becomes a "junior Enki" of the younger pantheon—a god of water, irrigation and fertility, while also the god of arcane knowledge, oral tradition (unrecorded history) and scribal writing. He is the *Mardukite* "God of Writing" (the "Divine Scribe" or "recorder") and inventor of the reed stylus pen, which allowed for a Babylo-Akkadian refinement of cuneiform script and a standardization of its styling and small characters—the earlier primitive version being inscribed using fingernails and such.

Under the ancient epithet Tutu, he was a reality engineer—a divine artificer and creator—often depicted holding the *Tablet of Destinies.* As such he is the inspiration for the original iconic archetypes behind the *Tahutian* (Thoth) and *Hermetic* (Hermes) wisdom traditions outside of Mesopotamia. In fact, as Thoth, Nabu is one of the few deities directly appearing in the ancient Egyptian pantheon that was not from Egypt. After Babylon made a premature attempt at supremacy in *c.* 3750-3450 BCE, *Mardukite* culture was mostly suppressed during the Sumerian era. Therefore, much of Nabu's pre-Babylonian activity leading up to the *Age of Aries* occurred outside (west) of Mesopotamia.

Much like his father, Nabu continued to more additional titles and his literary-cult gained wider influence as the *Age of Aries* progressed. One of the Neo-Assyrian period warlord kings, Ashurbanipal (*c.* 660 BCE) fancied himself an intellectual and went on to establish the largest royal library of his time in *Nineveh* (called *Ninua* at the time, or *Kuyunjik* today), collecting every writing (or proper copies thereof) in the known world. He was particularly interested in having information from every single Babylonian tablet that could be found and even dedicated his entire library to Nabu.

From letters concerning Neo-Assyrian temple officials and a certain sacred ritual involving Marduk, Nabû and Tašmetu, in the words of Nabû-šumu-iddina (SAA 13 78: 11-21), we read:

> *ana bulu napšate ša mar šarri belija*
> *lušallim u lepušu /*
> *minu ša mar šarri beli išapparanni /*

Bel Nabû ša ina Šaba u hašaddašan
uni napšate ša mar šarri belija liṣṣuru /
šarrutka ana šat ume lušalliku

"For the sake of the life of the crown prince, my lord,
they should perform the rites of their gods to
perfection.
What are the written instructions of the crown
prince, my lord?
May Bel and Nabû who are betrothed in the month of
Shebat,
protect the life of the crown prince, my lord.
May they extend your kingship to the end of time."

TRIADS OF BABYLONIAN DEITIES

THE SUPERNAL TRINITY
ANU + ENLIL + EA/ENKI
{Heaven + Air-Space + Earth}

THE WATCHERS IN THE SKY
NANNA + ISHTAR + SHAMMASH
{Moon + Venus + Sun}

THE HOLY FAMILY OF BABYLON
MARDUK + SARPANIT + NABU
{Jupiter + Mercury}

IMPORTANT CITIES OF THE GODS

"Nippur was not made; E-kur was not built.
Erech was not made; E-anna was not built.
The abyss was not made; Eridu was not built."
[CT. XIII, Tablet 82-5-22, 1048. Plate 35, ln. 6-8]

The first city-states in history developed and spread around a central Temple. While many early homes in Mesopotamia were crafted from reeds and mud, the most permanent structures (for those that could afford it)—such as the Temple District —were constructed of sun-dried clay bricks. Of course, we must say "most permanent" because the long-term survival of these structures without continuous repair was anything but permanent—as the ruins which litter the "Middle East" today would suggest. Kiln-fired and glazed bricks were not commonly used in construction until the Babylonian Renaissance.

Impermanence of early Mesopotamian construction contributed to the appearance and mystique that it later gained at the height of its various eras. Archaeologists often had difficulty in properly dating various aspects of these sites because of how frequently they were built upon the remains of preexisting ones—and this continued for thousands of years, essentially raising the terrain of urban areas like hills set against the otherwise flat environment. As the earliest Temples and Palaces were repeatedly rebuilt over time, their elevation especially towered over the city.

Entire scholarly volumes are dedicated to archeological details of Mesopotamian city-states. Here, we are concerned with formally introducing just a few specifically that most affected the complete Babylonian legacy.

ERIDU

{ *Modern Site: Abu Shahrain* }

> *"A reed had not come forth,*
> *A tree had not been created.*
> *A house had not been made,*
> *A city had not been made,*
> *When all the lands were sea,*
> *Then Eridu was the first city."*

E.RI.DU (or NUN.KI) is the very first known prehistoric Anunnaki settlement in Mesopotamia, settled long before the "Deluge" and predating any established system of writing and civilization there. Some called it "City of the Tree (or Palm)," "The Good City," "The Home Far Away" and "The Deep." Its origins became legendary once history was recorded—for it was not only the oldest, but it was the home of Enki. In a short time, it became a major religious center at the southern most point of Mesopotamia.

Excavated remains of Eridu extend as far back as *c.* 5500 BCE (as the "Stone Age" ends); though archaic tablet writings—and the famous "*King Lists*"—suggest an Anunnaki presence there for much longer. For example, Eridu is the location serving the first two "legendary" proto-Sumerian kings—Alalum and Alagar—who ruled before the "Deluge" with a reign that spanned *thousands* of years. To put into further geographic perspective: the ancient city of Ur was established only fifteen miles northeast of Eridu.

As the legend goes, when civilization was first started (or restarted, depending on your view of prehistory), Enki (E.A./Ea) the *apkallu* ("wise sage") rose up from out of the Persian Sea (now the Persian Gulf) and established his home right on its coastal shores. From there he dispensed wisdom, knowledge, and the "Arts of Civilization." This legend survived many millenniums. The *Mardukite* historian Berossus (*Bel-re'u-sunu*, High Priest of Marduk's Esagila, *c.* 250 BCE) writes of it (in the Greek language of the Hellenistic era) where *Oannes* (*U'anna*), the fish-god, emerged from the Persian Gulf and taught humanity the "*Epic of Creation*" (*Enuma Elis*).

During ancient periods, the Tigris and Euphrates rivers each independently flowed into the gulf, where today they actual converge into a single river before reaching the sea. The Persian Gulf is now nearly one hundred miles away from the ancient site of Eridu, but this was not the case thousands of years ago. The gulf has since "shrunk" in size, leaving behind a marshy silty wetland where the sea once was. The receding waters may have resulted in more land area today, but in *c.* 5500 BCE, Eridu would have been the southernmost point of Mesopotamia along the Euphrates, right on the coastline of the gulf.

Excavations at the site reveal that it originally consisted of a single small structure with a single room—the original home (or shrine) of Enki—measuring a mere 12 feet by 15 feet. This simple temple had only one main doorway leading to a single altar-table in the center and a niche in the wall where a statue may have stood (but which has never been found). These are the humble beginnings from which the *Mardukite-cult* was born. But things did not remain so humble.

By the proto-Sumerian Ubaid period of the early Fourth Millennium BCE, the Temple of Enki had grown tremendously. It now featured a design that would become a basic template for temples and churches ever after: a large hall with many separate cell-like rooms on either side—and at the far end of the hall, the sanctuary-shrine was elevated as much as forty feet high on a terrace (accessible by a stairway).

BABYLON

{ Modern Site: Babil }

Most academicians and historians begin their account of Babylonian history with the First Dynasty of Babylon *c.* 1900 BCE. And it is true that this is when the *"Amorites"* (*martu, amurru*) or ancient *Mardukites* finally established the supremacy of Babylon for the *Age of Aries*—effectively replacing the old Sumerian "lunar cults" and "elder" version of the Anunnaki pantheon. However, archaic tablets suggest that the actual site of Babylon had already existed, extending back into prehistory. The *Amorites* (or *Mardukites*) spent two centuries infiltrating Mesopotamia with a goal to directly reach and reclaim Babylon. They did not arbitrarily just decide to establish their new dynasty and thriving metropolis there by chance.

Modern *Mardukite* tradition includes esoteric lore that is not necessarily accepted or agreed upon by other contemporary academic sources. A summary of this controversial *Mardukite* and Babylonian prehistory is included in the 'Introduction' of "*The Complete Anunnaki Bible*":

"The mission to unify all of civilization under a *'Mardukite'* banner (to return people to the Source through 'magic' and 'prayer'; not animal and other sacrifices of life, or wretched systematic enslavement) did not bode well for the other gods. Marduk sought to bring the *'Navel of the Earth'* from antediluvian Nippur to Babylon during the *Age of Taurus*. But his 'Star-Gate' at BAB.ILI (*Babylon; "The Gateway of the Gods"*)—the original *'Tower of Babel'*—was destroyed in *c.* 3460 BC. Marduk then went to the Nile Region—where he was known as RA—and a 350-year war between gods ensued there for supremacy before Marduk returned to Mesopotamia for the *Age of Aries."*

Marduk's great *ziggurat* of *Babylon-city* was named E.TEMEN-AN-KI – *Etemenanki*; "Temple of Heaven and/on Earth" or "Temple of the Universe" or "House of the Foundation of Heaven and Earth," &tc. It towered 300 feet tall in seven stages, starting from a 300-by-300 foot base. Each of its rising stages or levels were accessible by a ramp-like staircase from the preceding one. The sacred "House of Marduk (and Sarpanit)" was at the very top. It is the proverbial "*Tower of Babel*" of legendary renown—built, destroyed, then rebuilt, several times over the course of thousands of years.

The *ziggurat* was off-limits except to clergy and deities. Others seeking to worship or petition the gods would go to the more publicly accessible "Temple of Marduk (and Sarpanit)" called E.SAG-ILA (*Esagila*; "Lofty House," "House of the Lofty Head" or "House That Lifts Its Head")—which was also found in the Sacred Precinct or Temple District that extended 40-60 urban acres at times. Excavations reveal that the "Temple of Marduk" alone measured 470 feet on its longest side (with a total square area much larger than a modern city block). Within the Temple, the shrine of Sarpanit was located in a special "cell" or room called *E.dara-anna*.

BORSIPPA

{ *Modern Site: Birs Nimrud* }

Borsippa not only served as the sacred precinct of Nabu and Teshmet, but also was the quintessential college-town of *Mardukite Babylonia*. Located ten miles south of *Babylon-city*, Borsippa was the official home of Nabu and Teshmet, their sacred cult-center, seminary, convent, scribe-school, astronomical observatory, and the Great Library of Babylonia. There is evidence of its occupation from at least the Third Millennium BCE, predating the First Dynasty of Babylon (much like the site of Babylon itself).

Ruined remains of the central *ziggurat*—E.ZIDA —still rise 150 feet above the surrounding landscape today. Presumably it was a half-size model of Marduk's great E.TEMEN-AN-KI in Babylon. While little more than a mound and crumbling tower is found there now, it is still more visibly intact than most other ancient sites in that region— perhaps living up to its namesake of "Enduring House" or "True House."

Early academic archeologists of the 19th Century knew the general area to look for ancient Babylon, but not its exact location. When they first began to excavate Borsippa, scholars actually believed they had found Babylon—and even the surrounding populations held a belief that the towering remains were, in fact, the famous "*Tower of Babel.*" But, of course, they were wrong—and the actual site of Babylon was finally discovered nearby in the 1880's.

URUK (ERECH)

{ *Modern Site: Warka* }

Inclusion of Uruk is unique for our brief study of Mesopotamian cities, because it was not a *Mardukite* center (unlike Eridu, Babylon and Borsippa). It was, however, prehistoric—established on prehistoric and archaic Anunnaki roots—just like the previous sites. Originally it was the sacred city of Anu (and Antu) at the apex of the proto-Sumerian pantheon—but it was soon "gifted" to the goddess Inanna-Ishtar. Combined, Anu and Inanna were the central deities of its spiritual tradition.

Early foundations for Uruk's sacred precinct were constructed along the Euphrates River in the late Fifth Millennium BCE, approximately 60 miles north of Enki's spiritual center in Eridu. It remained mostly a small cult-center until *c.* 3750 BCE, when Mesopotamian culture shifted from the proto-Sumerian "Ubaid" period to the proto-Sumerian "Uruk" period. This transition also coincides with the beginning of the "Bronze Age." [We say "proto-Sumerian" because the early dynastic period that is historically referred to as "Sumerian" really begins *c.* 2900 BCE—at which point there are many city-states throughout Mesopotamia, each ruled by their own dynasty (until they were unified by the Akkadian Empire).]

Esoteric *Mardukite* lore explains the sudden rise of Uruk (and the diminishing cultural significance of Eridu) with a narrative regarding the Anunnaki god Enki and the goddess Inanna-Ishtar. In one version, she gets him drunk; in another, she seduces him. The truth probably lies somewhere in between. But, most importantly, Inanna-Ishtar is able to relieve Enki of the sacred *ME*, the "discs" containing data for the "Arts of Civilization" and other details regarding the systematization of reality. She takes these with her to Uruk and suddenly many of the historical "firsts" are implemented and spread as "civilization."

It is from Uruk that Inanna's "fertility-cult" originated and soon after became a staple of ancient Mesopotamian religions. It is during this period that we find the first ritual expressions of "sacred marriage"—symbolically recognizing a "divine union" between Inanna and her new lover, Dumuzi (*Tammuz*). Uruk is the City of Ishtar that "Gilgamesh" (*Bilgames*) is the King of in the classic epic. Events recorded as Ishtar's "Underworld Descent" likely took place during the Uruk period too.

In the beginning of a lament of Ishtar's for her lost city she lists temples and cities by name.

"My faithful house, my E.mahtila,
My faithful house, my E.temenanki,
My faithful house, my E.dara-anna,
My faithful house, my brickwork of Uruk,
My faithful house, my E.anna,
My faithful house, my E.gipariminna,
My faithful house, my brickwork of Zabalam,
My faithful house, my Hursagkalamma.
My faithful house, my E-turkalamma."

"As for the lord, in his dirge, he has become
alienated from the house of Nippur from the
brickwork of Ekur, from the Ki'ur, the Enamtila
and the brickwork of Sippar, he moved away, the
whole land is in confusion. From the sanctuary
Ebabbar, the Edikudkalamma, and the brickwork of
Babylon, he moved away, the whole land is in
confusion. From the brickwork of Esagil, the
sanctuary Eturkalamma and the brickwork of
Borsippa, he moved away, the whole land is in
confusion From the brickwork of Ezida, from the
sanctuary Emahtila.
the brickwork of Etemenanki the sanctuary
Edara'anna
he moved away; the whole land is in confusion."

AN ASSYRIAN LITANY OF GODS

"You are sworn by Aššur, king of heaven and earth!
As well by Anu and Antu!
As well by Illil and Mullissu!
As well by Ea and Damkina!
As well by Sin and Nikkal!
As well by Šamaš and Nur!
As well by Adad and Šala!
As well by Marduk and Zarpanitu!

As well by Nabû and Tašmetu!
As well by Ninurta and Gula!
As well by Uraš and Ninegal!
As well by Zababa and Babu!
As well by Nergal and Las!
As well by Madanu and Ninĝirsu!
As well by Humhummu and Išum!
As well by Girra, by Nusku!
As well by Ištar, Lady of Nineveh!
As well by Ištar, Lady of Arbela!
As well by Adad of Kurbail!
As well by Hadad of Aleppo!
As well by Palil, who marches in front!
As well by the heroic Sebettu!
As well by Dagan of Musuruna!
As well by Melqarth and Eshmun!
As well by Kubaba and Kurhuha!
As well by Hadad [of ...]
and Ramman of [Damascus]!"

⚜ 3 ⚜
PRIESTS, PRIESTESSES & TEMPLES

"A Priest or Priestess is always to observe the pious ways and the Sacred Rites at the Altar of Offering."

THE RISE OF 'CHURCH AND STATE'

Prehistoric roots of Mesopotamian society—and all civilization thereafter—began approximately 8,000 years ago. By this, we mean what directly became "modern" civilization. Archaic tablets records also indicates nearly half-a-million years of Anunnaki activity on Earth, so we are not disqualifying much earlier societal "attempts" and long-lost civilizations and other sites that may be found.

When someone refers to Mesopotamia as the *"cradle of civilization,"* they mean the literal birth of specific systems of civilization that we now take for granted today as being simply common-place to any typical "human society." While some key factors of societal function have merely evolved with an increased population and physical technologies, other aspects have shifted or changed so significantly that they are difficult to accurately conceive of today. This allows us to challenge some of the commonly accepted academic and archaeological interpretations when shaping a "modern-day" *Mardukite* tradition.

A modern practitioner must take a holistic approach to conceive the wide-angle view that is ancient Mesopotamia—particularly concerning its origins and development, which have been obscured by time and miscommunication. At its start —even before "*kings*" and "*empires*" as we would understand them today—there was no separation of "*church* and *state*" (as they were one and the same entity). What's more: there we find absolutely no distinction between practices of "*religion* and *magic*"—and any such distinctions may really be the result of outsider interpretation anyway.

In short: the concepts of *religion*, *government* and *magic*, all began synonymously as a single systematization or paradigm of "human consciousness." And this impression or imprint on consciousness was installed directly by the Anunnaki Gods— whatever their actual nature may be; whether visitors from outer space, avatars from another dimension, or survivors of a previous advanced civilization—it really makes little difference. The results were the same: *Sumerian civilization.*

These details, and many others, are important for a "practitioner" of the tradition. For modern purposes, we mean specifically an "<u>esoteric</u>" *insiders* understanding as maintained by the "clergy" themselves—the priestesses and priests of the tradition. Even in ancient times, this "esoteric" understanding would have been superior to the "<u>exoteric</u>"

perceptions held by the general population. It is not surprising then that we find the priestesses and priests as the original "authority-figures" at the inception of human systems.

In previous chapters, we introduced Enki's *Eridu* as the prehistoric model for pre-dynastic proto-Sumerian culture. What developed into the first "city-state," really began with a "god" and his "home"; then grew into a "temple" for a "divine couple"; and then the world's first great institution for magic, science and religion—the "knowledge of the gods" and the "arts of civilization." All the while, rule of the area rested with Enki directly; then Enki *and* Ninki. But, shortly thereafter we find the very first class emerge that is separate from both "gods" and "humans" (and acting as a direct intermediary between them)—the *High Priestess* and *High Priest* of the Temple.

TEMPLE ROLES & HEIRARCHY

"Give dedication and commitment to the Eternal Source. Love one another; do not sacrifice animal life —but celebrate life and sing praises.
For there is no religion higher than the Source."
—Nabu-Tutu Tablets (Esoteric Series-T)
"The Complete Anunnaki Bible"

Although the word *"en"* later came to mean

"lord," it originally implied a *High Priest*; the word *"entu"/ "entu(m)"* indicated a *High Priestess*. For the original ancient tradition: Enki and Ninki were respectively the first *High Priest of Earth* and *Mistress of Earth*; they established the example or "order" that would be followed by those chosen to represent them to the people. As the local population grew and the social and political affairs became more complex, everyday management of the Temple itself might be turned over to official administrators called *"sanga"* (in Sumerian) or *"shangu"* (in Akkadian)—which means a "bound priest" or one that is fully "duty-bound" to their deity. After Eridu, this same pattern resulted in the formation of several other early city-states throughout Mesopotamia.

For present purposes, we will use the term "priesthood" to denote the class and religious order of both priestesses and priests (in place of the term "clergy"). The Temple-priesthood was divided into three main groups (or classes): the uninitiated ones; the initiated ones with limited privileges, and the initiated ones with full rights. For females specifically, there were five primary roles or functions: *"holy sister,"* *"priestess,"* *"hierodule,"* *"dedicated-woman"* and *"temple-maiden."*

Before long, dozens upon dozens of various titles developed to distinguish specific offices and roles of the many priestesses and priests of the Temple.

Most of them lived full-time at the temple complexes, serving the patron gods and performing religious—and sometimes medical—services for the inhabitants of these *Cities-of-the-Gods*. Unfortunately, many scholarly translations simply reduce all of the various titles to simply mean "priest" without understanding their function. But today we know that each meant something unique, such as the *erib biti*, or *"Temple-Enterer."*

The term *erib-biti*—or *Temple-Enterer*—denoted the highest level of priesthood; its members enjoying unlimited access to the Temple District. For example, the actual "shrine-cell" or "cella" was the most protected area of the Temple—of which only *erib-biti* were allowed to enter, and hence their name. Other ritual specialists, the cult-like staff of *šangû* and *ahu rabû*, lamentation hymnists, might have had access—and others, such as goldsmiths or textile workers that maintained the cult statues. For the most part, only those initiated or requiring access to the *cella* (and by extension, the courtyard to reach it), were allowed to pass.

Only initiates were allowed to serve in the Temple-courtyard. Such restrictions were necessary to prevent any "polluting of the offerings." The courtyard included another unique feature of religious significance we might recognize today as a *baptismal-font*, or *tank* containing an accessible supply of standing *"holy water."* In Babylon, this special basin of holy water symbolically called the *abzu* or *apsû*—reflecting the significance of the "deep waters" of Enki's Sea, or even the "Abyss."

Other specialists within the priesthood included:

patesî, nisakku or *issaku* — "high priest"

nu-es — "exalted priest"

pasisu — "anointer" (responsible for purifying persons and objects with sacred oils and pure waters)

asipu, īshippu, zammeru, and *kalŭ* — "wizards" (skilled in "magical arts")

makhkhu — "great one" (a subset of *asipu*)

issipu or *baru* — "soothsayer" (seer/diviner)

nisakku, ramku, or *surmahhi* — received offerings and divined the will (generally the material and dietary needs) of the temple-god(s)

dashishu, mahhŭ, or *hărŭ* — "guardians of the oracle"

kali or *galli* — "eunuch-priests"

masmasu — "ritual assistant"/"purifier" (officiate)

zammaru — "chanters"

isqu — "novitiate" (an apprentice)

Above all else, the chief religious and social function of a priestess (or priest) is to act as the mediator between a deity and its worshiper. They were a distinct high-class of citizen, living in and serving the sacred precincts. These "Temple Districts" grew into large cult communities (on their own) within the greater urban sprawl; and much like government infrastructure today, they required their own secure vested specialists to perform the common everyday tasks.

To be a *"Priestess of Marduk"* (*entu* or *sal-me*) in Babylon required being *ellu*, "clean" or "pure"— or sometimes translated as "blameless." This meant physical cleanliness and grooming, even proper lineage or descent, *&tc.*; but also (and perhaps more importantly) indicates emotional and psychological clarity. Priestesses were often responsible for dispensing counsel and spiritual advisement—after first having received an appropriate regimen of this themselves.

In Sumerian, KAR.KID is usually translated as *"Daughter of God."* This title carried a similar meaning as *hemet neter* or "consort of god" in the Egyptian tradition. And like *the* Sumerians, Babylonian priestesses adopted a new name when officially initiated/ordained. Some classes of priestess could marry and even be a stepmom. For example: a *nadītu* (like a "nun" or "sister" today) of Marduk could marry and have sex, but could not bear children. In this case, a designated *Šugǐtu* (or second wife) could have the man's children, so that the *nadītu* could lead a "pure" and "flawless" life. According to the *Code-of-Hammurabi*, those who dared to touch or kiss a *nadītu* could be burned to death. To approach or even dream of one might warrant punishment.

THE PATH OF THE TEMPLE

priest	priestess
boy	girl
shows talent as scribe/priest	wants to be priestess
literary education	literary education
difficult training	difficult training
great rewards	great rewards
god/goddess	goddess/god

TASKS AND RESPONSIBILITIES

The *en* and *entu* had many duties. They conducted religious rituals and brought offerings to the altars of their Gods. Tending to the altars and shrines included ritual washing, anointing or cleansing of the space and statuary, and any ceremonial setup. They managed the Temple District, performing purification and healing rites, community rituals and seasonal festival ceremonies. They managed urban affairs, helping to keep law and order in their cities. They even had their own military—the very first organized factions of guards and warriors. They sang hymns of praise and played jubilant songs. They promoted fertility in the land, among animals, and the family unit. They were expertly trained in the sexual arts and offered many counseling services at the Temple.

COMMUNICATION
CARE AND FEEDING OF GODS
SERVICE TO THE GODS
OFFERINGS TO THE GODS
RELAYING PRAYERS AND ANSWERS
INSTRUCTING IN PRAYER
PURIFICATION AND EXORCISMS
MEDICAL TREATMENT
MUSIC / SONG / HYMNS

BASIC ATTIRE

"Priestly" or ritual attire distinguished a member of the priesthood from others in the community. It also served a psychological function for the practitioner themselves—for by donning the sacred regalia of their office, the individual also recognized themselves as a representative of the "deity." In time, this was symbolism was equally transferred to represent the power and authority of the "state." And as we have previously suggested, the two were soon identified as one and the same in social consciousness.

Typically the priesthood wore white—but many dressings including ornamental accents and features, sashes, worn seals and other indications of one's position or office. Priestesses often word "flounced" robes and attire—where additional material is attached, or else the material along horizontal seams are gathered up to add more "frill" and "body" to an otherwise "straight" appearance.

It was considered unclean or "impure" for the soles of the feet to touch the ground, so all initiates wore sandals of various designs. A priestess also adorned her head with an *aga*—or else what we might call a "tiara" today. When they died, priestesses and priests were buried with the attire and symbols of their holy office. They were also buried with other golden objects—crowns and rings—intended as gifts or "dowry" to their deity. These tombs were located in a place called "The Hall Which Brings Sorrow."

ALTAR RITES

"To Speak As One With The Gods,
I ___, Entu of ___ ..."

If a Temple represents a microcosm of the Universe—a smaller version of the same—then an *Altar* is specifically symbolic of the relationship between the "deity" and the "Universe." Likewise, we might say that any religious or spiritual practices involving the altar also represent direct relationships between the "deity" and "self"—and between "self" and the "Universe." The nature of these interactions is what became "*tradition*"— symbolically represented as "*religion.*" There is also a possibility that construction of some primitive altars imitated an obscure archaic "control board" or "communication device" that originally served even more "practical" or "technological" functions—which may have only been properly understood by the "*gods.*" At present, we are most concerned with their traditional religious use.

We have briefly mentioned the "altar" previously —an upright standing object at, or upon which, the "sacrificial" offerings (mainly food and other fine items) are made to the Anunnaki Gods (and other "spiritual" entities). Babylonians constructed altars from any available materials, including: reed, clay, brick, wood, or precious stones inlaid in gold. At the prehistoric Temple of Eridu, its small shrine first consisted of an altar set into a niche in a wall opposite the doorway. That, combined with a small offering table in the center of the room, completed the simple devotional area of the very first "sacred space" dedicated to an Anuunaki-based religion.

Various emblems and symbols—specific to the tradition or a particular deity—might also be present, either inscribed (or painted) on the altar, or as objects set upon or near it. For example: an altar may be placed on, or next to, a statue of a deity's sacred animal—or, a large enough "statue" of the god's animal could serve as an altar, which the symbolic objects and offerings placed on its "back." The "sacrificial meals" were placed on the altar—or near it, on a pedestal or other basket-like container. Meals consisted of a two-course breakfast in the morning and then a dinner late in the day.

Some basic symbols one might find associated with a Babylonian altar (as appropriate for use by a priestess), includes: the solar disc, "horned" cap (representing the Moon), a "spade" (sacred to Marduk), a sign that resembles the Greek "*Omega*" character, a sign for the "*Aries*" constellation, &tc. There are many items one might place on or near the altar, depending on one's intention (or prayer) or nature of the rite, such as: a favorite rock, incense, candles, statue(s), and bowls of various oils.

There are several factions of the priesthood that made regular use of the altar. *Baru* divined the will of, and consulted with, the gods. They also studied the skies for changes and motions; watched bird flight patterns; looked for patterns in smoke and oils dropped in bowls of water—in general, they looked for, recorded, and monitored *patterns*. Records of these observed patterns resulted in the first types of divination and omens. They essentially served as "soothsayers" and "seers" for the

Temple and state.

If we classify the *baru* as a seer, then an *asipu* is a wizard. The *"ashippu"* (or IŠIPPU) priests were also spiritual healers, and often responsible cleansing or sanctifying the temples and shrines. They performed the "incantations" and "exorcisms" (such as in the *maqlu*, *surpu* and *utukku* rites)— and developed *amuletic* plaques to ward the walls and doors of a Temple (and of which were also used frequently in personal homes). They studied divination, dream interpretation, necromancy, and magic. They operated as conjurers, diviners, and enchanters. [In the Temple-District, *Bit-assaputi* means "House of the Oracle," so named from the *"asipu"* root.]

Asipu also made *"house-calls."* This required setting up an "offering table" or "reed altar" (if one was not already present in the dwelling). Sometimes, these *"traveling asipu"* would carry kits that included material to make temporary makeshift altar-shrines. Offerings were made as part of formal religious rites—but these rites also included physical treatments and herbal medicine. *Sabatu* is the act of purifying the area a ceremony is to be held —whether at the Temple or some other designated "sacred space."

Dramatic ritual elements supplemented other physical care, adding a spiritual and psychological component to the healing arts. Incantations were used—usually describing a narrative whereby some god visited some higher god for advice—relaying instructions and setting the tone for "magical work." This directly encouraged a patient to better "get themselves well" or reinforced stronger "belief" in the effectiveness of a physician and their actions. This component is still found today in among modern "health-care" practices, though it is seldom spoken of. Far from primitive, ancient Babylonians even recognized and treated such things as "situational stress," "mental disturbance" and "psychosomatic illnesses."

When an *asipu* made any petitions to a deity (regardless of the type of "magic" they conducted), a small "sacrificial meal" would be offered (and each deity invoked would get their own portion) on or near the altar. The meal typically consisted of small breads—preferably those baked with "fine white flour" (*isq-ūqu*)—vegetables, dates, meat, and a *mersu*-confection (made with ghee and honey). A couple *la'annu*-jars (of water, beer, wine, cow milk) were poured out into an *adagurru*-vessel or *pursıtu*-vessel set out to hold the "libation." [A libation might be either poured out onto the ground (if purely symbolic or appropriate) or poured into a waiting vessel.] During the meal, censers are lit, filling the area with the fragrance of juniper and/or cypress burnt on *asagu-*

146

thorn charcoal. A seating area may be indicated with a *misu*-cloth. Once meal preparations are complete, the *asipu* leaves the area (so that the god can eat in peace). Upon returning (after 10-20 minutes), they present offerings of cedar and/or silver.

CONSECRATING & ANNOINTING

"Consecration"—or the act "to consecrate"—is a religio-magical term meaning "to purify and make holy or sacred." Traditionally, only an initiated member of the priesthood could do this—someone with proper training and skill to "*direct intention.*" All ritual implements, all sacred objects in the Temple, and all offerings made to the Gods, required formal purification or consecration.

We briefly mentioned the *abzu*-font, which held "*holy water*" (blessed by a priest/ess) in the Temple courtyard. Any water intended for such purposes would first be collected from an appropriate source—preferably from "running" (moving) streams and rivers. The "holy water" could also be bottled and dispensed for individual/personal application; but most commonly it was used to "bless" large areas and congregating crowds—lightly sprinkling (flung from a distance) using an *asperges/aspergillum* tool (or dried palm leaves).

To bless water—which is to say "make" *holy wat-*

er—an ancient tablet fragment instructs gathering seven sacred plants/herbs (the specific varieties are unknown today), which are set in a bowl of water for three days. Then, the following incantation is repeated three times before the bowl.

> "Pure water;
> Water from the Euphrates;
> Water which has been kept
> aright in the Deep,
> The pure mouth of Ea (Enki)
> hath purified it.
> The Children of the Deep,
> Seven are they.
> They purify the water,
> Cleanse it, make it limpid;
> Before your father, Ea (Enki);
> Before your mother, Damkina (Ninki).
> May it be pure, be bright, be clean;
> That the evil tongue may stand aside."

Where a congregation or gathering is concerned: *kinetic motion* is a readily available "tool" (or social catalyst) for raising energy, programming energy, and releasing energy. By this, we mean ritual dance (and music) employed for consecrating and "charging" spaces, sacred tools, the people themselves, and other things present. At festivals, it was used for "raising spirits." They held hands and danced clockwise in a circle to build and focus their energy. You can easily imagine a group of beautiful girls holding hands, dancing in a circle, combining their energy like bright orange cords of light. Then the churning clockwise motion would "spiral" the energy up and out.

Fire is also used for ceremonial purification. It is the central component of the "burning rites" or "*maqlu ritual*"—which are described in a companion volume of this series.[*] But incense smoke (made from blending wood, herbs and/or oil) is present in nearly all Babylonian rites. Whether simply present or burned, most of the sacred Mesopotamian "herbs" and "essences" (cedar, cypress, juniper, frankincense, myrrh, *&tc.*) were believed to have "purifying" properties.

Fresh herbs and essences are preferred whenever used for ornamental altar dressings, incense resins, and when making oils. Some deities favored certain substances, which could affect what essences and oils might be most appropriate for a particular rite or petition. For example: *tamarisk* is sacred to Anu; *cedar* to Ea/Enki; *acacia* and *juniper* to Inanna/Ishtar; *myrrh*, *lotus* and *belladonna* were popular among priestesses serving a goddess.

---

[*] "*The Maqlu Ritual Book*" (in hardcover), simultaneously released (in pocket paperback) as "*Anunnaki Rites: The Maqlu Ritual Book*." Some of the information previously appeared as the *Tablet-M Series* in "*Complete Anunnaki Bible*."

Oils were used for consecrating, anointing and specialized forms of divination. Olive-oil, or any "natural oil" (*vegetable*, *coconut*, *grape-seed*, *&tc.*) or "fat" may be used—either by itself or as a base for an herbal infusion. One one archaic tablet, the recipe for "dream oil" (or "prophet oil) is given. A single batch calls for one half-cup of *olive-oil*, a pinch of *cinnamon*, a pinch of *nutmeg*, and a teaspoon of *anise*. You then: 1) heat and strain the combined ingredients; 2) pour into a clean jar; 3) anoint/apply to the forehead and temples; and 4) store away from heat, light and moisture.

The following incantation may be applied whenever oil is used to anoint an individual—either for healing purposes or as a general blessing for religious rites:

"Pure oil, clear oil, bright oil,
Oil that purifies the body of the gods,
Oil that soothes the sinews of mankind,
Oil of the incantation of Ea (Enki),
Oil of the incantation of Asalluḫi (Marduk).
I coat you with soothing oil
That Ea (Enki) granted for soothing,
anoint you with the oil of healing,
I cast upon you the incantation of Ea (Enki),
lord of Eridu, Ninšiku.
I expel Asakku, ahhāzu-jaundice,
and chills of your body,

I remove dumbness, torpor
('lethargy' or inactivity),
and misery of your body,
I soothe the sick sinews of your limbs.
By the command of Ea (Enki), king of the apsû,
By the spell of Ea (Enki),
By the incantation of Asalluḫi (Marduk),
By the soft bandage of Gula,
By the soothing hands of Nintinugga
And Ningirima, mistress of incantation.
On *so-and-so*, Ea (Enki) cast the incantation
of the word of healing
That the seven sages of Eridu soothe his body"

THE 9 PLACES OF ANOINTMENT

1. THE SOLES OF THE FEET

2. THE BENDS OF THE KNEES

3. THE BASE OF THE SPINE

4. THE GENITALS

5. THE WRISTS

6. OVER THE HEART

7. THE BREAST

8. UNDER THE CHIN

9. THE FOREHEAD

SHRINES

Descriptions for the design and function of a "shrine" is found throughout this book. It is listed here in this chapter among other specific "tools" or "components" of religious-magic and the tradition practiced by priestesses and priests of the Temple. However, "personal shrines" were also found in most Babylonian homes, dedicated to both "personal gods" and "ancestral spirits" (departed loved ones and family members).

Design of a shrine ranged from quite elaborate to the most simple—an image and a candle to illuminate the area at night. A shrine might also contain statues, *steles*, and/or basic tablet renderings. A special rug (or "prayer mat") might be placed on the floor; used for prayer and as a clean surface to kneel on. Shrines often included a small altar-like table, a wall-niche (or edge) to place an "offering-plate" (and candles).

By including incense smoke and resonant tintinnabulation of a brass bell, the personal intentions (petitions, communications) of the practitioner were carried up to the heavens. Items selected as an offering (and/or burnt as incense, *&tc.*) were based on personal preference—that of the practitioner and/or the "deity"/"spirit" being honored. [Below is a list of of commonly chosen offerings frequently recorded on relevant tablet records.]

FRUIT	NUT	GRAINS
POMEGRANETES	PISTACHIO	WHEAT
FIGS	WALNUT	SPELT
APRICOT	ALMOND	BARLEY
CUCUMBER	PINE NUT	CAKES
DRIED FRUITS		
DATES		
HONEY		

VEGGIES	LIQUIDS	OILS
LEEKS	DATE PALM WINE	SESAME
ONIONS	GRAPE JUICE	SAFFLOWER
GARLIC	POM. JUICE	ALMOND
ARUGULA	BEER	BALANOS
TURNIPS	WINE	CASTOR
		MORINGA
		POPPY SEED

MEAT	INCENSE	MATERIAL
PORK	FRANKIN.	MUSIC
SEITAN (fish)	MYRRH	STATUE
	GALBANUM	CLOTH
MUTTON	LABDANUM	COMB
LAMB	MASTIC	MIRROR
BEEF	CEDARWOOD	MONEY
	PINE	COMM. SERVICE
	LOTUS	
	LILY	READING
	FIG	
	ROSE	
	SWEETGRASS	

PHYSICIANS & HEALING

Many priestesses and priests specialized in the healing arts. Healing was, and remains, a trained skill. Its origins extend into prehistory. Any records of prescriptions originating in Eridu have never been uncovered. There are some basic cuneiform "medical textbooks" from the Sumerian period, but the Babylonians made many significant innovations. Assyrian King Ashurbanipal later collected all of these tablets to construct the most complete "medical library" of the Ancient Near East.

Archaic tablets describe two basic names for a physician. Unfortunately, academic scholars are quite confused about their distinction. On the one hand, we have the *asu*, meaning "physician" or "doctor" (not gender-specific); and on the other, the *asipu* (*ashipu*), primitively translated as "witch-doctor." Scholars believe that the *asu* focused exclusively on "physical" remedies, while the *ashipu* applied only "spiritual" ones. This was not the case. Both types applied "holistic" treatments as the situation required. The only real difference is that the *asipu* was also clergy—part of the Temple staff—and more expertly trained.

Learned Babylonians understood how certain "physical" symptoms generally required "physical" treatments—but they also believed that the visible or obvious "physical" manifestation of many ailments possessed underlying "spiritual" causes. In fact, the oldest records describing heart-break, mania, depression, emotional health, and psychosomatic effects, are all written in cuneiform.

A professional healer was required to make initial preparations for healing rituals, which an *ashipu* used when applying spiritual and/or physical treatments. Preparations for such a rite included: preparing libations; purifying the "clay pit"/arranging magical encirclements; making and dressing any surrogate figurines, laying out sacred objects, medicinal tools, and herbal ingredients; and finally, helping the patient to ready themselves (both physically and psychologically) for the ritual. [The patient was also instructed to make petitions/prayers to their personal deities.]

Babylonian physicians utilized spiritual knowledge, prayer, magical encirclements, and administered amulets during healing rites. But on a physical level, they also worked with purifying fumigants, linen-bandages, herbal pharmaceuticals, salves/ointments, potions/tinctures, topical washes, hot-baths, suppositories—and even enemas. The formal nature of a healing ritual contributed to increasing the "faith" or "belief" that the patient had for the procedures (medicine) and skill of the physician; therefore willingly participating "psychologically" as a critical component of the personal healing process.

For most basic applications, cuneiform tablets provide simple procedural instructions describing the deliberate actions made by a physician or *asipu*. It always began by purifying one's self—as is still the standard medical practice today. Herbs and other ingredients were freshly procured. A circle was drawn on the floor with fresh flour. Incantations were recited. Offerings and libations were made to (appease or pacify) the relevant deities. Figurines are held up to the gods. Fumigants were burned. Injuries are washed and dressed. Salves, potions, and other herbal pharmaceuticals were applied.

Fumigants

Fumigants were applied when treating many common complaints—most notably: headaches, gastrointestinal discomfort, ringing of the ears, shortness of breath, a stiff neck, vision issues, and other "unspecific" ailments. The ingredients are collected, crushed (or ground), and/or mixed with a flammable substance, before burning on hot coals. An incense burner (censer) is often, unless directed otherwise as specified on the tablet (for example: using a human skull).

Bandages

Clean linen, cloth, or leather bandages were applied alongside other topical treatments. The

skin is lubricated to prevent drying. Herbal/
mineral ingredients are crushed and sifted—then
soaked in *kasû*-juice, beer, wine, milk, vinegar, or
urine (or a combination of these). If it is too wet,
flour may be sprinkled on top before applying the
bandage, which may be heated or chilled as the
situation required. A bandage is applied directly to
the hurt area—wherever the "ghostly pain" afflicts
the patient. For headaches: the bandage is wrapped
around the head or temples. For an earache: bound
around the ears.

Salves

For medicinal salves and ointments: ingredients
are mixed with an oil (usually cedar), animal fat,
resin and/or wax. The specific tablet instructs the
healer to char, crush, or grind them. The mixture is
often allowed to sit overnight. To ensure that
medicinal properties of the salve would penetrate
the skin when rubbed on the patient, ancient
Mesopotamians included purified crushed stone
grit. As with bandages, they are applied directly to
the affected area. In addition to "normal" topical
applications, special salves were used to treat ver-
tigo, shortness of breath, neurological disorders,
and other "unspecific" ailments. [The following
list is applicable for bandaging instructions as
well.]

Headache salves — rubbed on the temples/eyelids

158

Eye salves — daubed on eyelids
Neckache salves — rubbed on neck/body/both
Ghostly pain salves — rubbed on sore area
Internal pain salves — rubbed on abdomen
Fever salves — rubbed on head/soles of the feet
Salves to guard against apparitions — rubbed on
   the head and soles of feet before getting out
   of bed

Most ingredients used to make salves are not considered "magical" in nature, unless their intended purpose is "magical." For example: the magical formula for a *"spirit-apparition salve"* required "dust from a human skull." It is also important to note that salves that have "magical" purposes (such as *"to guard against apparitions"*) are the only ones that *require* a simultaneous offering-rite during preparation—since they pertain directly with the domain of the "spiritual" world. A tablet-fragment reveals part of the instructions, as given here:

"burāšu-juniper and red salt
   you mix in erēnu-cedar oil
repeatedly rub it on the foot and head"
—or—
"burᵃšu-juniper, kikkirānu [...]
   grind together
   mix with aromatics
repeatedly rub on the bottom of feet"

Pharmaceuticals and Potions

Medicinal tablets recovered from the royal library of the Assyrian King, Ashurbanipal, reveal that ancient Mesopotamians assigned medicinal properties to an estimated *120* "mineral" substances and *250* "herbal" ingredients—specific barks, flowers, fruits, leaves, roots, *&tc.* Today, scholars are still working to properly identify many of the transliterated names for these. Ancient names for *sulfur* and *alum* are found in many healing formulas—as are *potassium nitrate* (an astringent) and *sodium chloride* (an antiseptic).

Many identifiable medicinal "herbs" mentioned on cuneiform tablets are quite recognizable to modern herbal practitioners today, such as: *asafoetida, belladonna, cannabis, cardamon, cassia, cinnamon, coriander, date, fig, fir, garlic, henbane, juniper, licorice, mandragora (mandrake), mint, mustard, myrrh, myrtle, pear, poppy, thyme*, and *willow.* Urban "healing centers" (the Temple) would have maintained a supply of both fresh and dried ingredients—which required either growing them locally or importing them.

Potions, tinctures and extracts were used to treat many of the same ailments as bandages and salves, and were frequently combined with such treatments. Ingredients might be ground, crushed, or sifted—then if necessary, refined further overnight in water or vinegar. Once strained, evaporated, and powdered, the final product was commonly dissolved in, or mixed with, *beer* for consumption (preferably on an empty stomach)—although *honey*, *milk*, or *wine*, could also be used.

Washes

A "wash" serves both physical and spiritual purposes. On a practical level, it is intended to cleanse and purify the body—or an area of the body—prior to other treatments. [Though in some cases, it may be the treatment for a specific area or affliction.] A wash is applied to the body from the top, moving downward, to prevent contamination. [This is opposite from the practice of anointing with oil, which is applied from the bottom, moving upward—to avoid it dripping on an "un-anointed" area prematurely.]

Ingredients are ground and mixed with pure water, oil, or a combination of oil mixed with other liquids. Washes were used to treat "flashes" in the eyes, "roaring" in the ears, and even gastrointestinal distress, among other things. When indicated, liquid mixtures were poured onto, or blown into, an orifice using a straw (a hollow reed or metal tube)—and/or a lower-body soak-bath might be prepared. These types of treatments are most frequently mentioned on tablets describing certain "venereal diseases"—literally "*Venus diseases*" or being "*touched by the hand of Inanna-Ishtar.*"

Note this fragment of a diagnostic tablet:

> "If blood flows out of the penis, it is the hand-of-
> Shammash;
> a sign of the Underworld (Land-of-No-Return).
> If the penis and testicles are inflamed,
> the hand-of-Inanna-Ishtar has reached him in his bed.
> If the testicles are inflamed and penis is covered in
> sores, he has gone into the high priestess of his god."

Suppositories

The ingredients were ground or crushed, sifted, and wrapped in a tuft of wool. This was formed into a finger-shaped pellet using sheep fat. Before being inserted they were lubricated with *erënu-* cedar resin. Suppositories were used to treat "roaring" or inflamed ears (when caused by a blockage it served the same purpose as a cotton-swab) and gastrointestinal discomfort. Enemas could also be included in this category. The ingredients are baked or boiled in beer or urine, filtered, then allowed to cool before use.

SEERS & DIVINATION

> "The Observation of Oil in Water;
> The Secret of Anu, Bel, and Ea;
> The Secret Tablet of the Gods,

The Sachet of Leather of the
Oracles of Heavens and Earth;
The Wand of Cedar-Wood
That is Dear to the Great Gods..."

Divination is an esoteric/arcane skill, or mystical art, concerned with "divining" or "discerning" future events or consequences. Babylonians believed a "seer" or *baru* (meaning "inspector" or "one who examines") could literally "see" the future—or that which is otherwise not visible or perceived by that normative senses of the '*Human Condition*'. And while such beliefs are commonly reduced to party-trick fortune-telling and generalized horoscopes today, ancient Mesopotamian society was extraordinarily dependent on specialized clergy that were effective and well-practiced in *divining* the "will" of the gods.

The obvious root of the word "*divination*" is "*divine.*" This denotes recognition of a personal relationship between "humans" and "gods"—or between "earth" (*physical*) and "heaven" (*spiritual*), and how the two are affected by each other. Material (*earthly*) success was thought to be dependent upon direct cooperation of the gods (*the spiritual/metaphysical cause*)—and their "will" (*Cosmic Law*). This "*divine knowledge*" was sought by priestesses and priests serving as *seers.* [All clergy were required to maintain some level of communication with the *divine.*] Their function was to act as a mediator or interpreter between the deity and the worshipers in order to ensure that the worshipers may obtain guidance in the personal matters of their every day life.

All priests and priestess were trained to deliver petitions, prayers and requests *to* the gods. Even the average citizen in Babylon could accomplish this to some degree. But *seers* and *"diviners"* specialized in mediating (relaying) messages *from* the gods. The Babylonians believed that one's destiny was "written in the skies." They studied the systematic movement of celestial bodies, meteors, and constellations—ascribing to them names (and attributes) of their Anunnaki gods. As such, *true astrology* was born. They were particularly interested in observable patterns of the "wandering stars" that so strongly influenced activity on earth —which we call "planets" today.

Seers and "divination-priests" *looked* for "signs" of the *divine*, often called *"omens."* They documented systematic patterns in nature, where something was observed to precede the occurrence of something else. They interpreted these *omens* according to records of the past, assuming a principle that "like-circumstances would bring about a like-result."

Archaeologists have recovered literally thousands of cuneiform *"omen tablets"* filled with "if such-

and-such, then such-and-such" statements. Ancient "diviners" used this information to guide interpretation (and predictions) of unforeseen changes in nature, the varying appearance of the heavens, and unstable phenomena on earth. It was also used to determine "auspicious timing" for all significant matters of state and military, when certain actions would more favorably lead to a particular desired outcome.

Babylonians recognized two main classifications of divination—roughly translated as "voluntary" and "involuntary," but of which we might consider "intentional" versus "conditional." In the first type, "voluntary" acts of divination involve the *seer* or *diviner* personally and intentional *seek out* some sign or use some object or other medium as a catalyst. For the involuntary type, the "*baru*" observed *conditional* factors and features that manifested unbidden (as if "omens" sent by some god), and in any event *demanding* interpretation.

VOLUNTARY/INTENTIONAL DIVINATION
- *Observing drops of oil in a bowl of water*
- *Interpreting "tea-leaf" remains in a cup*
- *Casting sticks, staffs, rods, and "drawing lots"*
- *Casting bones and "drawing stones"*
- *"Bibliomancy" using cuneiform tablets*
- *Interpreting "dice rolls"*

INVOLUNTARY/CONDITIONAL
DIVINATION

— *Observing positions of stars and planets*
— *Destructive tornadoes (violent storms)*
— *Interpreting patterns and motion of clouds*
— *Swarms of locusts (insect pests)*
— *Interpreting flight-patterns of birds*
— *Deformities and health in livestock (cattle)*
— *Birth of twins, triplets, &tc.*

Dream interpretation might apply to either type—
but "voluntary" only if the *prophetic dream* is
intentionally sought out, such as described in
Silvestro Fiore's *Voices from the Clay*:

> "*Oneiromancy* is a favored means of
> knowing the future at the time of Gudea
> [*c.* 2150 BC]; the *en-si* [transliterated from
> the logogram PA-TE-SI] went into the
> temple with an intention of dreaming 'in
> the god's abode' and gaining knowledge
> of 'Divine Will'. Assyrian kings some-
> times sent 'Dreamers' into the temple,
> whose dreams were then interpreted as if
> experienced by the sovereign himself. It
> is possible that the dreamer partook of a
> narcotic potion, before lying down to
> sleep, in order to be favored with a div-

ine message. Many of the dreams favored
as omens by the Mesopotamians needed
interpretation, since their purpose, 'to reveal the god's intention' was not always
clear."

THE TEMPLE DISTRICT & ITS STAFF

The main subject of this book is the religious (vocational) life among Babylonian clergy—and
many details seem to overlap between sections and
chapters throughout. Here, we will close this
present chapter with a concise summation of principle details regarding the Temple-District and its
staff.

The "Temple-District" served as the 'chief edifice'
of all Mesopotamian cities; a central conglomera-
tion that not only ran a city's business affairs and
facilitated it's daily life, but were also cared for by
the people of the cities they helped thrive. Cities
usually had multiple temples, each one dedicated
to a particular deity. Smaller sanctuaries within a
temple were also dedicated and consecrated as
spaces to serve 'related' deities. For example: the
E.SAGILA temple in Babylon-city dedicated to
Marduk also contained a separate sanctuary for his
consort, Sarpanit.

Temples prominently became the focus of urban

religion. They drew the public to congregate in their outer courtyards, typically sectioned off from the surrounding area by a wall. An inner-courtyard or *kisallu*, existed on the other side of the large wall—considered off-limits and practically non-existent to the "uninitiated." Various other areas of the Temple-District were also restricted to specific grades or classes of clergy.

As an economic (corporate) identity, the Temple was the wealthiest financial institution in ancient Mesopotamia—yes, even surpassing that of the "Palace-District" and the king. The Temple owned one-third of all real estate in Babylon. And since most Mesopotamian cities developed as a response to strong founding religious-center, the Temple was the *oldest original* land-owners, and generally took possession of the "best" properties available. They also owned and managed their own livestock (cattle) and gained revenue from endowments and voluntary offerings. They were also the primary money-lenders, with an ability to fund projects and endeavors far greater than any private merchant.

Even apart from specific "offerings" made to the gods, the concept of "tithing" (ESRÂ) originated in Mesopotamia—a form of payment made to support the Temple (by its congregation). This gratuity was a spiritual and civic duty, practically a "religious tax" collected from the urban community, which in return received material support, counsel and protection from the Temple (a tradition that began long before dynastic kings or a political military). Even after the prominent rise of palace-kings, bureaucratic systems, aristocrats and armies, the Temple still served as the primary civic-social governing institution for this religio-centric culture.

Far from public participation in the outer court-yards, the "innermost sanctum" or "Holy of Holy" (*paraku*) of the Temple was curtained off and re-served especially for its patron god—or an appropriate embodiment thereof, referred to as the "*cult statue*." This was the most important religious "symbol" in Babylonia.

The "*cult statue*" was not simply a "representation" of the deity—such as one might find in their home for a personal shrine. After appropriate consecration and dedication, the *cult statue* of the Temple was considered *to be* "same-and-as" the deity (when otherwise absent). This later gave rise to varying misconceptions regarding "*idol worship*" by outsiders (uninitiated).

Once they were materially created, *cult statues* required consecration and dedication through a series of evening rituals where they were given "life"—their mouth "was opened" (*pet pî*) and "washed" (*mis pî*) so they could see and eat. If the deity approved of its consecrated form, it would accept the "image" and agree to "inhabit" it. A similar "opening of the mouth" rite was used in Egyptian tradition—where the clergy would wash, anoint, pray over and consecrate the statue intended as a physical vessel for the deity.

Last, but certainly not least, in this department: the *ziggurat* of each Mesopotamian city was also built within the Temple-District. Its prominent appearance, visible quite far away, was perhaps the most significant religious symbol. Standing tall, like a mountain peak, among an otherwise flat landscape, these massive multi-tiered buildings became the most famous icon of ancient Babylonian religion. Clergy would ascend its many stairways and levels in imitation of their own spiritual ascension, but also to conduct rituals, recite prayers, sing hymns of praise, make offerings to the shrine (at the top), and make astronomical observations.

The Temple was also the largest employer, requiring many skilled-talents and individuals performing *dullu*—"service to the gods." There were herdsman, butchers, millers, oil-pressers, brewers, cooks, bakers, servers, accountants, treasurers, scribes, messengers, janitors, guards, artisans, weavers, tailors, seamstresses, barbers, singers, acrobats, gatekeepers, candle makers, and reedworkers.

⚜ 4 ⚜
SYMBOLS, TOOLS &
MAGICAL RULES

*"At the command of the Lord and my Lady,
may what I am doing be successful."*

ANCIENT SYMBOLS

Initial development and later advancement of human civilization—and its systems—was dependent on the establishment and communication of "*symbols*." Symbols are (usually) abstract representations (or substitutions) for a *person, place, thing, concept* or *idea*. Symbols become "*tools*" when they are used to relay a shared-meaning between two or more parties/participants. For example, all writing systems are based on symbols with a "shared-meaning" assigned to them. In fact, it is the shared understanding and native use of a certain *language*, far more than geographical location or genetic-ethnicity, that archaeologists use to distinguish one ancient culture from another. Symbols are the very seed from which *culture* grows.

Symbols also become *tools* when an individual uses them intentionally to "evoke" or "conjure" the representative (prescribed) meaning in their own mind—or when treated as an indicator of something personally significant. For example:

performing divination; interpretation of dreams; making amulets and sacred implements/tools; incorporation into sacred art; marking property (*kudurru*-stones); and interpreting "omen" signs observed in naturally occurring patterns and manifestations of everyday life.

Ancient Babylonian "Symbols of Power" (generally representing some "divine" or "heavenly" aspect) were used for legal and/or religious purposes. For example: deity symbols (identified with captions) were placed on *kudurru*-stones, which marked real-estate boundaries and royal land grants. Clay images (figurines) of deities and other beneficent spirits were inscribed with incantations for "magical spells." Celestial and "*zodiac*" symbols were considered as powerful as the original deities they represented. The *apkallu* are representative of the *divine sages* (which are treated as ancient protective guardians)—depicted as griffin-like creatures—as featured on tablets and artistic reliefs, each holding a "pine cone" and a "bucket." [Many other significant symbols are listed throughout this section/chapter.]

"*Letters*" (as symbols) and "*numeric sequences*" have served an *oracular* function in *divinatory* systems, for many thousands of years. In fact, while the Babylonians continued to refine their *cuneiform script*, they continued to treat the ancient Sumerian characters (of their Mesopotamian predecessors) with sacred reverence. Symbols, let-ter-characters and images representing various concepts are given preassigned meaning, then drawn "randomly" and interpreted. The most obvi-ous examples still in use today are "*runes*" and "*tarot cards.*" In the past, various oracular symbols have also been placed on tiles, clay coins, and even sticks. Almost any material can be employed for these purposes.

NUMERIC SYMBOLS

Numeric symbols representing the Mesopotamian "base-60" mathematical system are represented by *cuneiform script*. The number "*1*" is represented by a single wedge-shaped mark. The remaining numbers through "*9*" are simply composed of indi-vidual marks collected in groups. [Seven "*1*" marks equals "*7.*"] A separate single sign existed to represent "*10.*" [The original ancient system did not have a "*zero.*"]

In many ways, signs for larger numbers are cumu-latively arranged in a similar fashion to "Roman Numerals"—where the value "*25*" (or "XXV") is represented by *two* signs for "*10*" ("X") followed by a "*5*" ("V"). In Babylonia, you would use *two* "*10*" symbols and *five* "*1*" symbols. One unique peculiarity of the system is that "*60*" is simply rep-resented by a slightly larger version of "1"—a

single *cuneiform* mark. The value of "75" is written by starting with a larger single mark, followed
by a "10" sign and *five* "1" marks.

[Less frequently, the "*minus*" sign was used at the
end of a number (to lower the total value represented). This means "9" could be written as a group of
nine "1" marks, *or* as a "10" plus a "*minus-1*."
Therefore, *subtraction* notation in math calculation
first began as "adding a negative value."]

𒐕 1	𒐏𒐕 11	𒐎𒐕 21	𒌋𒐕 31	𒐏𒐕 41	𒐎𒐕 51
𒐖 2	𒐏𒐖 12	𒐎𒐖 22	𒌋𒐖 32	𒐏𒐖 42	𒐎𒐖 52
𒐗 3	𒐏𒐗 13	𒐎𒐗 23	𒌋𒐗 33	𒐏𒐗 43	𒐎𒐗 53
𒐘 4	𒐏𒐘 14	𒐎𒐘 24	𒌋𒐘 34	𒐏𒐘 44	𒐎𒐘 54
𒐙 5	𒐏𒐙 15	𒐎𒐙 25	𒌋𒐙 35	𒐏𒐙 45	𒐎𒐙 55
𒐚 6	𒐏𒐚 16	𒐎𒐚 26	𒌋𒐚 36	𒐏𒐚 46	𒐎𒐚 56
𒐛 7	𒐏𒐛 17	𒐎𒐛 27	𒌋𒐛 37	𒐏𒐛 47	𒐎𒐛 57
𒐜 8	𒐏𒐜 18	𒐎𒐜 28	𒌋𒐜 38	𒐏𒐜 48	𒐎𒐜 58
𒐝 9	𒐏𒐝 19	𒐎𒐝 29	𒌋𒐝 39	𒐏𒐝 49	𒐎𒐝 59
𒌋 10	𒎙 20	𒌍 30	𒐏 40	𒐐 50	

For religious-magic purposes, a number might also
be used to represent a specific deity (as a substi-
tute place holder or even an esoteric formula for
its name). A tradition began during the Sumerian
era where key figures of the Anunnaki pantheon
are given a numeric designation. This eventually
inspired prescribing additional mystical "corres-
pondences" to numbers (based on a deity's personality or the planet they represented), establishing

the earliest known system of abstract "*numerological*" interpretation (used for divination, tablet records, and magical spells, *&tc.*). [Values assigned directly to Anunnaki gods are given in a previous chapter.]

CELESTIAL & ESOTERIC SYMBOLS

The following list includes the *most* common imagery and symbolism depicted (or described) on cuneiform tablets, clay amulets, religious statuary, and relief art. [When appropriate, a corresponding deity name is also provided. Note that the consort of a listed deity is likely also being represented.]

- 'Ankh', AN-KI (see *Rod and Ring* and *Beetle*)
- Arrow, Bow (*Ninurta; Marduk*)
- Beetle, Scarab* (*immortality, longevity, wisdom*)
- Bull, Heavenly (*Anu*)
- Bull (*Bel – Enlil*; also *Adad*)
- Cane, Crook (*divine guidance, shepherding*)
- Cone, Pine (*divine blessings/intervention*)
- Crescent, Moon (*Nanna-Sin*)
- Crescent and Disc (*Nanna-Sin* and *Ningal*)
- Crown or Helm of Horns (*Anu*)

---

* The *scarab* is a sacred symbol in both Egypt and Mesopotamia.

- Crown, Royal (*Bel – Enlil* or *Marduk*)
- Cutter, Umbilical (*Ninhursag*)
- Date/Palm Trees (*agricultural deities*)
- Disc, Sun (*Shammash* and *Aya*; also *Marduk*)
- Disc, Winged (*divine, Sun, Nebiru; Marduk*)
- Dog, Domestic (*Bau-Gula*)
- Dots, Seven (*the planet Earth*)
- Dragon, '*mushushu*' (*Marduk* and *Nabu*)
- Eye (*deities/divine, Anu, the Sun/Shammash*)
- Fish (*Ea-Enki*)
- Fish-Man (*Ea/Enki*; and the city of *Eridu*)
- Goat-Fish (*Ea/Enki*; and the city of *Eridu*)
- Lamp, Oil (*Nusku*)
- Lightning (*Enlil, Ninurta, Adad* and *Marduk*)
- Lion (*Inanna-Ishtar*)
- Rod and Ring (*divine power, cosmic authority*)
- Rosette and Star (*divine wisdom*)
- Snake, Serpent (*Ningishzidda* and '*genetics*')
- Spade (*Marduk*)
- Staff, Serpent; '*caduceus*' (*Ningishzidda*)
- Star, General (*skygods/deities, spiritual*)
- Star, 4-points, and rays (the *Sun, Shammash*)
- Star, 6-points (*heaven-earth union, Marduk*)
- Star, 8-points (*skygods/heaven, Inanna-Ishtar*)
- Stylus, Reed (*Nabu*)

- Sun Disc (*Shammash* and *Aya*; also *Marduk*)
- Tablet, Cuneiform (*Nabu*)
- Trident, Forked (refer to '*Lightning*')
- 'Tree of Life' (*systems: cosmic, spiritual, life*)
- Trees and Ibexes (*fertility, agricultural deities*)
- Turtle (*Ea/Enki*; and the city of *Eridu*)
- Vase, Water (*irrigation, Ea/Enki*)
- Waves, Water (the '*Waters of Life*', *Ea/Enki*)

SYMBOLS OF "THE SEVEN"

References to "*The Seven*" are found on many Mesopotamian incantation-tablets. They are presumed to be seven specific deities or ancient guardians, though interpretations differ on their identity. However, representative symbols are given for "*The Seven*" on one obscure tablet fragment. We can decipher these symbols as: a *fox*, a *dog*, a *raven*, a *vulture*, a *non-coyote-wolf thing*, a *raptor-bird*, and a *crocodile*. The original tablet reads as follows:

> "*A fox with a sweeping tail;*
> *A thing that sniffs around like a dog;*
> *Something pecks at caterpillars like a raven;*
> *A giant carrion-eating eagle;*
> *A non-wolf lamb-eating creature;*

A thing that screeches like a hawk;
And a shark in the waves."

OTHER TABLET FRAGMENTS
(DESCRIBING SYMBOLS)

"The Sages (*apkallû*)
with the faces of birds, and wings,
carrying in their right hands
a 'purifier' (*mullilu*),
and in their left a bucket (*banduddû*);
or another pair of Sages
cloaked in the skins of fishes..."

* * * * * * *

"...the seat and horned crown
of *Anu*, king of heaven;
the walking bird of *Enlil*,
lord of the lands;
the ram's head and goat-fish,
the sanctuary of great *Ea-Enki*..."

* * * * * * *

"...the sickle, water-trough
(and) wide boat of *Nanna-Sin*;
the radiant disc
of the great judge *Shammash*;

the star-symbol of *Inanna-Ištar*,
the mistress of the lands;
the fierce young bull of *Adad*,
son of *Anu...*"

CHECKLIST — PRIESTESS TOOL-KIT

Generally speaking, the supplies and consumable materials required by a priestess (or priest) to participate in the Babylonian religious tradition (and/or practice its "magic") would be provided for by the Temple. Basic descriptions of the tools appear in various chapter-sections of this book wherever specific instructions call for them (or where matters of the Temple, &tc. are described). However, modern practitioners likely do not have access to a proper Babylonian Temple. Therefore, in order for you to experience this tradition as originally intended (and as described within this book and related *Mardukite* literature), some of the most critical items for you to collect are listed below.

[ ] Censer, Vessels, Vials

Uses: aroma/ambiance; offerings (incense carries prayers skyward); burning releases energy (from the material/substance; area purification; personal purification.

Materials: bottles of perfume, scented oils, anointing oils; containers of herbal incense.

[ ] Jars, Bowls, Aspergillum

Uses: holding, preparing, and sprinkling blessed waters.

Materials: dried palm leaf; jars; bowls; spoons/ladle.

[ ] Oracular Divination System

Uses: to divine the unknown, or discern answers.

Materials: drops of oil in water (in a bowl); incense (smoke); telescope (astronomical observation); 'lots' – reed straws, twigs, dice, coins; clay tiles (with symbolic runic glyphs/characters inscribed thereon).

[ ] Candles, Lamps, Torches

Uses: ambiance/light to work by (illumination); presence of the sacred fire (element).

Materials: plates with sand or candle holders; charcoal (for censer), flint and tinder (matches or a refillable windproof oil lighter).

[ ] Sacred Art, Statuettes, Reliefs

Uses: focal point; representations of personal god and goddess; presence of the earth element (clay and other substances).

Materials: image of deity(s); statuette; wood, glass, clay; photo, drawing; any deity-specific symbols.

[ ] Blessed Flour

Uses: marking space (boundary of magic circle on the ground); protection/safety; directing energy ('magic dust').

Materials: pouch containing blessed clean fine-white flour (called 'Flour of Nabu and Teshmet'; or on instruction-tablets from Sumerian tradition, 'Flour of Nisaba').

[ ] Magic Carpet

Uses: a barrier between clean garments and the ground; portable consecrated space (for offering rites and incantation-prayers); an area for setting out tools and materials; meditation; 'astral travel'.

Materials: a square or rectangular 'prayer rug' or moderately-sized carpet (handwoven and consecrated).

[ ] Sacred Tablets

Uses: recitation of prayers/incantations; instructions for offering rites and rituals.

Materials: clay tablets (or in modern times, books and scrolls, &tc).

[ ] Ritual Attire / Clothing

Uses: dressing; status/class; rank (in the priesthood); protection; cleanliness (appearances).

Materials: robe, cloak/mantle, conical hat,

tunic, skirt, belt-cord, scarves, sashes, diadem, earings, bracelet, necklace (amulet), sandals.

CASTING & DRAWING LOTS

The term "lot" (as in "lottery") denotes *random selection* from a group. When we say to someone, *"well, that's your lot,"* we mean *"that's what you're getting"* as in the result you are *"allotted."* In ancient Latin, the term is *sortes*, the root of "sortition" (the practice of randomly selecting a representative or political official). The tradition actually extends into Anunnaki prehistory (as recorded after-the-fact). According to cuneiform tablets: *Anu, Enlil* and *Ea-Enki* original chose their positions (or celestial domains) by "drawing lots"—randomly selecting from three different lengths of reed-straw or stick-twigs (which have been the archetypal standard ever since).

Many different kinds of object can also be used to advance a similar type of *cleromantic* divination system. And over the course of thousands of years of human history and cultural variation, just about every type of material and representative-form *has* been used—marked scarabs, painted tiles, beads, buttons, sea-shells, bones, and dragon tears[*] (just to name a few). The only real rules for divination

---

[*] Specifically *Dragon's Blood* – a dried palm-sap resin commonly melted on hot coals for incense.

are quite basic: preassigned meaning and random selection. Even the act of "flipping a coin" to assist with making a decision is ancient in origin and falls neatly into this category.

Dice were also commonly used for divination. This practice is traditionally known as "*astragalomancy*" today, because many ancient dice discovered by anthropologists and archaeologists (among various cultures) were actually made from certain bones. However, in Mesopotamia, dice were manufactured from clay—and they were usually *four-sided*; tetrahedral, not cubed. Such dice have been found along with boards to play the "*Game of Twenty-Squares*"—sometimes referred to as the *Royal Game of Ur*, due to its initial discovery while excavating the ancient city.

The most basic form of dice divination is rather like "flipping a coin" to determine "YES" and "NO" (based on "odd" or "even" resulting values). In one Babylonian version, two dice could be rolled. The first represented the "past," while the second one equaled the "present." Then the two were added together for insight on the "future." [*e.g.*, *past* plus *present* equals *future*; ($X+Y=Z$).] To advance this concept further, a third aspect may be included to indicate "MAYBE" (as indicated in the following *Table* and *Activity* based on cuneiform records).

YES	NO	MAYBE
WHITE	BLACK	GREY
HEADS	TAILS	X
ODD	EVEN	X

As a general rule: a single set of '*lots*' (whatever material type they are) is stored in a small pouch. Following the advice from elsewhere in this book, a priestess (or *seer*) would cleanse, pray, meditate, and focus on the question or issue at hand. The question is whispered over the bag (sometimes three times). Then, with eyes closed, they reached in, and pulled one element out for interpretation (or else drew them one at a time, if called for, as the case may be.

ACTIVITY

In this activity, you are invited to make your own basic set of *lots*. To begin: choose a material that is readily accessible and to your liking (whether sticks, stones, buttons, *etc*). You can always make more than one set (to experiment with) later on, making each from a different material. Use the guidelines and *Table* in this chapter to assist you.

For our illustrative example, we will use the three stones that the author found on a nature walk. Three of the same color, size and weight were chosen—essentially indistinguishable from each other when felt inside a bag-pouch. Since the stones in this example are the same color, the author added basic symbols for "indicators." With a gold-colored permanent marker, they drew an "X" on one for "NO"—and an "O" on a second for "YES" (and the third stone was left blank as the *gray* "MAYBE" aspect).

Then, they are placed in their own clean new pouch. The pouch and materials inside of it are purified, consecrated and blessed as a single unit. Use a preferred method or technique that you have already learned from this tradition. Then, pray, meditate and focus on the oracle. Whisper your question over the bag, close your eyes, draw your *lot*, and divine your answer.

Q1: _____

A1: _____

Q2: _____

A2: _____

WATER DIVINATION

The most basic method of "water divination" (or "pool divination") used in Babylon is performed by throwing a pebble into the water. Then you simply count the number of ripples or rings that appear. An *odd* number indicates "YES"; *even* is "NO." [In this wise, you can see how the simple *Table* given in this chapter may be applied to diverse applications.]

SCRYING

Scrying (or *skrying*) is the method of divination involving "gazing" or "softly looking" at something as a catalyst for "internal visions" and "insight." Alternatively, one might be looking for *patterns* within the medium itself. We will quickly illustrate these two different approaches in a basic example. If one were to use *fire* as the medium, then the hypnotic-trance state that one achieves by gazing into it can be a catalyst to inspire visions, *&tc*. Alternatively, one might also look for physically observable *patterns* within the activity of the actual flames, or even the smoke that trails up from them.

As with any form of divination in Mesopotamia, the practice is a religious rite (however brief it may be) and follows the basic "standard practices" previously described throughout this book. This includes various preparations and purification of self and the area, &tc. On a practical level, such rituals allow one to fully commit themselves to the "intentional act." Additionally, one might consecrate and anoint with oils to be in full spiritual receptivity of any "divine" messages and so forth.

There are many mediums available to a *seer* of Babylonian tradition: fire-gazing, watching clouds, observing motions of oil droplets in water, or meditating on some divine symbol. But, beyond any specific "technique" or medium that might be applied, the *real* practice for this skill mostly concerns increasing the ability to "clear" one's mind (or "*mind's eye*") and allow for naturally-occurring imagery or insight to arrive (rather than forcing it or creating it). This is not really achieved by book learning and study; it results only from personal practice and experience.

'CIRCLE-CASTING'

A '*magic circle*' for personal rites and rituals can be marked out on the ground with many materials, including (but not limited to): flour, stones, crushed rocks, salt, reeds, leaves, twigs/branches, and fire (made by encircling with alcohol and igniting it). In this wise, the *magic circle* is an abstract (and often impermanent) *tool* that was not included on the earlier "*tool-kit*" checklist. It is used for: centering or focusing; consecrating sacred space; spiritual protection; and as a preliminary to rites and meditation.

In view of the fact that "*all intentional acts are magical acts*" and "*magic and religion are one*" in Babylonia, there was no such thing as an "arbitrary" or "nonchalant" rite or healing or drawing of lots. A priestess or priest treated each activity (described in this book) as a sacred act. When performing rites, or intoning a prayer, the priestess was not alone speaking to themselves; they considered they were in the presence of their deity.

The gods expected to be treated as honored guests (even if only attending "in spirit"), invited only to the purest and most consecrated spaces whenever their attention was called upon. The ritual area was swept clean with a *palm-frond* (the original "broom") and sprinkled with water (to settle the dust). In addition to performing any personal preparations (purification, *&tc.*), a circle is visibly marked around the working area (which includes the bed or another individual in the case of healing). And as such, the *magic circle* is "cast."

It is important to note that the preferred material used for '*casting a circle*' is *blessed flour*; mentioned in the previous "checklist" as the '*Flour of Nabu and Teshmet*' (or '*Flour of Nisaba*' on older Sumerian tablets).

A TABLET FRAGMENT ON 'GESTURES'

> *"Lift hands upward—for a prayer;*
> *Cup upward—to bless and name;*
> *Palm outward...*
> *Holding the throat...*
> *Raise the staff—for strength;*
> *Strike the wand—for power and protection."*

AMULETS

While there is no literal word for "*amulet*" in Mesopotamia, many token objects (such as "*cylinder seals*") were used for this purpose, and so it is the label many historians and mythographers have applied to this area. Quite simply, for our present purposes, we will define an *amulet* as any object, a natural substance, creation or artifact, that is believed to possess magical and/or protective powers.

Amulets are either carried by a person or placed at the location of desired effect. They might bring good fortune, avert evil, or both depending on the intention placed into their creation and consecration. They are an example of (what anthropologists refer to as) "sympathetic magic"—deriving their power from connections with nature, from religious associations, and from the very rituals of their creation. Depending on their intended purpose, various ingredients—herbs, flour, ground-up stones and oils—might be mixed in with the construction materials and/or used to consecrate the object afterward.

One medical-tablet describes instructions for using a "healing charm" on a patient. Dip the (*amulet*) in oil and rub it on patient. Then, place it around their neck to absorb the particular "*ailment-entity*" (*spirit*, *ghost*) that afflicts the body. Then, place it in a leather bag. The leather material the bag is made from should be taken from an animal that has died of natural causes. Alternative, it may be wrapped in a tuft of wool (preferably red-dyed wool). This wool might also be smeared with cedar resin, cedar oil or other oils.

These healing "*amulets*" required appropriate names to be inscribed on them. They should also be threaded on a cord made from two contrasting colors (usually red and white wool) to indicate the desired separation between the patient and the "ghost."

During the Neo-Assyrian Babylonian Renaissance era, the kings and clergy often wore a necklace with small metal amulets representing various symbols of the gods (as personally selected by the individual). In this wise, *amulets* served as extensions of one's personality.

EXAMPLE:
"Carve an image of a sirrush-dragon onto a small slab of alalu-stone (for good luck)."

SIRRUSH — "A FUMING RAGING DRAGON" WITH A "HAIRY MOUTH OF FIRE"

'DUB.U.HI.A' – 'A TABLET ON HERBS'

Medieval-era *"sorcerers"* in Europe were known for concealing some ingredients of their 'magical' *formulas* with "code names." Ominous alternate names were often chosen to keep the "uninitiated" (unintended readers) from understanding and using them. We find evidence of this same practice in ancient Mesopotamia. This peculiar tablet fragment lists several "code names" along with their actual substance, serving as a critical *key* for deciphering true ingredients from obscure 'magical' *formulas*. Its reverse side gives an esoteric correspondence-list regarding parts (internal organs) of the body and the planets.

"A Snake's Head: *a leech*;
Blood of a Snake: *hematite*;
Lion Semen: *human semen*;
Semen of Nabu/Thoth/Hermes: *dill*;
Blood From A Head: *lupine*;
Blood of Hephaistos: *artemisia*;
Human Bile: *turnip sap*;
Fat From A Head: *spurge*;
but Blood of Porcupine
really means *from a porcupine*."

Heart — *Sun*;
Brain — *Moon*;
Spleen — *Saturn*;
Liver — *Jupiter*;
Gallbladder — *Mars*;
Kidneys — *Venus*;
Lungs — *Mercury*.

KNOT MAGIC

The oldest records of "*Knot Magic*" (also called 'Cord Magic' in some traditions) are found in the ancient Near East. Its practice may be found among both Babylonians and Egyptians. Preferably one uses a natural cord of wool or cotton, which may even be dyed a particular color to match its use. According to one modern esoteric interpretation: "knots are tied to ritually 'bind' or 'hold' a magical intention for immediate or eventual use; they may be untied to 'release' energy or when an specific 'activated effect' is desired."[†] But, ancient instructions are not necessarily this concise or consistent.

When used for healing purposes (and general well-being), the priestess (or priest) is practicing "transference magic." In this wise, the illness (and/or spiritual cause) is *transferred* and *bound* to the knots of a cord. [By its very nature, 'knots' are useful for all manners of "binding magic."] In addition to the cord-color, the *number* of knots used for a particular "spell" usually has some numerological significance; usually (but not always) an odd number—often *3*, *5*, *7*, or *9*—with *seven* being the most commonly employed.

One example we may draw from a tablet calls for

---

†   "*Arcanum: The Great Magickal Arcanum*" by Joshua Free.

making a cord-necklace or bracelet, which is then worn as a preventative health measure (or blessing), or it may be used directly as part of a healing rite. When making it, the names *ulud* and *lama* (male and female protective/guardian spirits) are evoked to observe. Its intended use/effect will determine the cord-color (if any). When applied for healing (or pain management) it is tied directly onto the affected area. Seven (or *seven times seven*) knots are tied, anointing each one with oil (along the way). The following tablet-incantation may also be recited with each knot:

> *"Marduk, the wise sage of the gods;*
> *Erra (Nergal), warrior of the gods;*
> *Išum, herald of the street;*
> *The Sebettu, spiritual warriors without equal;*
> *Have mercy on me;*
> *_____ , the offspring of my god,*
> *Your reverent servant."*

After tying the final knot of the cord, recite (the incantation above) and then add to it:

> *"Should protection be assured upon the wearer,*
> *they will sing your praises,*
> *for all time to come and to all mankind"*

From the *maqlu ritual text*‡ we find many referen-

---

‡   Refer to "*Anunnaki Rites: The Maqlu Ritual*

ces to "undoing the knots of others"—of the evil-doers and evil magicians. However, In one of its rites, an "image" (representation) of one's enemy (or a spell to be undone, or an evil spirit) is prepared as a *cord* with *nine knots*. An incantation-line is recited with each knot and then a final line prepares the "image" for burning.

"May the mountain cover you!
May the mountain hold you back!
May the mountain calm you down!
May the mountain overpower you!
May the mountain swallow you up!
May the mountain pass reject you!
May the mountain cliff kill you!
May the mountain wastelands make you thin!
May the [mighty] mountain avalanche fall upon you!
Indeed, you shall be shaken from my body!"

ACTIVITY
[Create Your Own Amulet]

Materials Required: (*in place of clay, try*) flour, water, salt, plastic bowl, herbs and oils, a pouch, a reed-stylus or sharpened stick.

1. Add the flour and salt to the plastic bowl.

Book" or the Tablet-M series given in "*The Complete Anunnaki Bible*" edited by Joshua Free.

2. Add in any dried herbs and oils, then stir.

3. Add in water and stir until you get a dough-like substance.

4. Form some into a ball the size of your palm.

5. Mold it into a flat rectangle shape.

6. Use your reed/stick to punch a hole through the top.

7. Use the reed/stick to mark out a keyword or name across the top and/or bottom.

8. Mark the central square area with an image/symbol of your choosing.

9. Allow to harden or bake; thread with a cord and place in a pouch.

⚜ 5 ⚜
PRAYERS, HYMNS & CHANTS

"PETU BABU TEMU"
Open the Gates of Understanding

INCANTATION TABLETS

The purpose of this chapter-lesson is twofold. Most obviously, we are introducing a sampling of actual prayers and hymns translated from incantation-tablets and other recovered Babylonian tablet-fragments. These may be directly used (where appropriate) in conjunction with other training and suggestions provided in this book. But, additionally, we want a reader to gain a basic understanding of the patterned design (or formula) that such historical incantations follow. In this wise, *new* personal prayers specific to personal purposes and personally selected deities can be *newly written* by the modern reader or priestess (while still retaining authentic guidelines of the original tradition).*

---

* A perfect example of a collection of incantations newly written for the modern Mardukite Babylonian tradition was published in 2010 by Joshua Free as *"The Complete Book of Marduk"*; also re-issued as *"Anunnaki Prayers: The Cuneiform Almanac (New Standard Zuist Edition)*; and excerpted as the Tablet-W series in *"The Complete Anunnaki Bible."*

There are many examples that could be given. In fact, there are many additional examples found in other *Mardukite* volumes within this series. Naturally, for the present book, we are focusing on the structure and design of prayers used specifically by clergy—priestesses and priests—of the Babylonian Temple. [There is more information on ceremonial-temple incantation-prayers in the next chapter.] Tablets that contain prayers to a specific deity are grouped together. Where a single incantation-prayer petitions multiple deities, the order in which the names appear is usually indicative of the spiritual hierarchy (regarding which deities are most "in one's favor").

An incantation-tablet may or may not include specific instructions. For example, with the *maqlu tablet series*: several tablets detail spoken incantations for dozens of individual rites, whereas most of the instructions are found on a separate final tablet in the series. Aside from a few specific "series" of tablets that have been excavated together and collected, most of the recovered incantation-tablets and fragments do not often provide much instruction. It has been assumed that such details would be instructed separately as part of the priesthood-seminary training (as with the progressive lesson-chapters of this present book). As such, a priestess (or priest) would already know how to apply them.

Although the terms are often used interchange-ably: *prayers* are *petitions* (on some level) and usually (but not always) contain an *invocation*; *hymns* are generally recited or sung in general cel-ebration or reverence of a deity and may contain an *invocation*, but usually not a situational *petition* or *request*.

Incantations are used to praise the gods, petition them for help, and as an affirmation of faith. People prayed for almost everything. They prayed for the diseased and sick, for family/ancestral spir-its, to remove guilt, for the destruction of their enemies, to deflect witchcraft, and achieve worldly success. *Hymns* and *chants* were commonly used to raise energy and as another way to commune with deities. In most cases, an *incantation-prayer* follows a threefold pattern:

First part – an address to (praise of) a deity.

Second part – a petition, request, or lament.

Third part – giving thanks/receive blessing.

Generally, lines *one*-through-*ten* are a direct invocation of the god; line *eleven* (or *one*, if no invocation is present) is where the petitioner states their name (and brief lineage) and describes their need or their complaint; and the conclusion of the prayer contains various petitions and gratuitous rhetoric. When deciphering academic records or raw tablet material, it is important to note:

The colophon-line is the title of the prayer,
INIM.INIM.MA SU IL.LA;
It commences with the phrase: DU.DU BI
(or *ipui innatu*, "do the following")

A *rubric* is the direction or instruction contained in a single line. This line is never found separate by itself, but immediately follows the *colophon-line* and precedes any other directions for the ceremony or ritual. [If the formula line "*lu ina KISDA lit ina SA.NA ipui*" appears, it refers to the manner in which the *preceding* incantation-prayer is to be recited.] In brief, these instructions all indicate that the incantation be recited simultaneous with whatever action(s) the ceremony/rite calls for. [The most common instruction being simply to "*perform the incantation*"—meaning also all accompanying actions.]

CEREMONIAL TABLET FORMULAE

Some incantation-tablets include several instructional lines after a prayer, which describes what should take place during a larger ritual or ceremony. Such directions are brief and simple for shorter/smaller rituals; and the more elaborate a ceremony is, the more elaborate the instructions. However, their design still follows basic formula-patterns.

EXAMPLE ONE
(*three lines*)
"the offering of incense;
the pouring out of a libation;
the reciting the incantation three times."

EXAMPLE TWO
(*three lines*)
"In the night before Ishtar thou shalt sprinkle a
green bough with pure water.
The [...] drink-offering shalt thou present. Seven
times the food shalt thou [...]
A [...] of incense shalt thou offer. Place thou
there a garment and a gift."
(cleanse the area, the offering/incense and gift)

EXAMPLE THREE
"directions for making certain offerings;
the commencement of an incantation."

EXAMPLE FOUR
(*two lines*)
"directions for ceremonies; commencement of a
second prayer or incantation."

PRAYER AND PETITIONING

*"Have mercy on me, and, O Lord, hear my prayer!
Destroy my foes and drive away the wicked!*

Never let there approach me the poisons,
the enchantments [...]: [...]!
[...] pity me and command favor!
O my god and my goddess,
may peace be my portion!
[...] may thy heart have rest,
may thine anger be loosened,
and do thou establish prosperity!
Thy greatness let me praise,
let me bow in humility before thee!"

EXAMPLE ONE

line one: the goddess (*Bilit*) is addressed;
the next line: the god (*Bel-Marduk*);
then: examples of the god's power and mercy;
then: stating the petition before deity(s).

EXAMPLE TWO

"petitioner states they have offered a present,
and poured out a libation;
and then prays for removal of their sorrow
and sighing for the length of their days;
concluding with the desire that to declare the
greatness of the god unto distant peoples."

ADDITIONAL NOTES ON INVOCATIONS

"Anu, above me, the King in Heaven;
Enki, below me, the Lord on Earth;

The power of Marduk is within me; It is not I, but Marduk, that performs the incantation."

Traditionally, a Mardukite "*priest*" conducts the (incantations) ceremonies as though they are the original "*high priest*" of *Eridu*-city—*Marduk* and *Nabu*—as an extension of the power passed to them by *Enki*. Here, the operator literally *invokes* or "*calls in*" that specific spiritual current or flavor of energy. The priest asks for the '*god-form energy*' (reportedly '*cherry-flavored*') and conducts the remainder of the ceremony *as* that requested *form*.

ADDITIONAL NOTES ON PURIFICATION

Prepare a bowl of fresh water; add oil and salt; add fresh herbs; Then pass your hand over the water and make your incantation-prayer. Flick the water (using your fingers or a plant) around the room and on yourself; rinsing your hands in water; finally pouring the remaining contents of the bowl into the earth. This same procedure is followed with sacred oil, but you can store it in a bottle (rather than pouring out an unused portion). Dip your fingers in herb-infused water containing also olive oil and myrrh. Water and oil may be dispersed by using the tamarisk branches, reed or a date-palm stalk. Salt is considered pure and sacred by itself (even without formal consecration). Fire can also be used to purify.

ADDITIONAL NOTES ON "THE RIGHT WAY"
(BASED ON BABYLONIAN NABU-TUTU TABLETS)

Worship your god daily—with offerings, prayers, and appropriate incense. Bend your heart to your god; to that which befits the office of your personal god—prayers, supplication, pressing (the hand to) the nose (as a greeting). Each morning, shall you offer up to your personal god. Then your power will be great; and you will, through your god, have enormous success.

ADDRESS TO THE SUPREME DEITY
(ASSYRIAN / NEO-BABYLONIAN)

"In the heavens, who is great?
Thou alone are great!
On earth, who is great?
Thou alone are great!
When thy voice resounds in heaven,
the gods fall prostrate!
When thy voice resounds in earth,
the genii kiss the dust."

TO THE CREATIVE GOD
(AKKADIAN / OLD BABYLONIAN)

"O lord of charms, illustrious one;
Who gives life to the dead, the merciful!

Thou who didst create mankind in tenderness;
Thy love surrounds us!
Oh wind! The merciful!
The god whose life establishes us! O lord!
In darkest strife,
Oh never may thy truth forgotten be!
May the race of (Akkad) forever worship thee!"

PRAYERS TO ISHTAR

"Queen of Heaven, goddess of the universe;
you are the holy one of women and men.
The one who walked in terrible chaos;
and brought life by the law of love.
And out of chaos brought us harmony;
and from chaos, she has led us by the hand.
Women of women, goddess with no equal;
she who decrees the destiny of people.
Highest ruler of the world;
sovereign of the heavens.
Goddess, even of those who live in heaven.
With Ishtar, there is counsel and wisdom.
The fate of everything,
she holds in her hand.
Joy comes from her every glance.
She is the power, the magnificence;
She is the deity who protects.

She is the spirit that guides;
be it maiden or mother,
women remember her, and call her by name.
Oh, Shinning One!
You stop the anger of all other deities;
You care for the oppressed and the mistreated.
Each day offering them your help.
You are the one who gleams the brightest
in the midst of all other deities."

* * * * * * *

*[A prayer containing an invocation of the goddess
and description of her power.†]*

"O Ishtar, heroine among goddesses!
Thy seat is in the midst of the bright heavens!
Thou are [...], and like the Sun-god [...]!
Lady of the sky, the mountains and the seas!
Thou [...] the handiwork of creatures of the
ground, thou beholds [...]!
Thou scatters the nations [...], thou directs [...]!
[...] all of them [...] creation [...]!
Thou, O Ishtar, are powerful and great,
And thy seat is in the midst of the bright
heavens!"

---

† *Kuyunjik* tablet #32 (*British Museum*); *K-
3358.*

PRAYERS TO TESHMET

"O goddess Tašmitu, whose command is
mighty!
Who causes her word to be obeyed, who
establishes [...]!
Who appeases the anger of god and [...]!
Who hears prayer and supplication!
Who accepts petition and sighing!
Oh seed of Izida (E.ZIDA),
House of the living creature of the great gods!
Queen of Borsippa, Lady of the Dwelling!
Oh lady Tašmitu, whose command is mighty!"

[*The petitioner prostrates themselves before the
(image of the) goddess; describing (and appealing
to) her merciful character (as giver of peace and
prosperity); once more addressing her by name;
then proceeds to make a request.*]

"O Tašmitu, goddess of supplication and love,
lady of [...]!
I ___, the son/daughter of ___,
whose god is ___, whose goddess is ___,
Have turned towards thee, O lady!
Hearken to my supplication!"

* * * * * * *

[*On the ceremonial tablet: the first line directs*

sprinkling of pure water; an offering of incense (of fyarru-wood); and a recitation of the incantation. The second directs to employ the knotted-cord rite (tying nine knots, one for each of the "May..." lines of the incantation.]

"Before Nabu thy spouse, the lord, the prince;
the first-born son of Isagila (E.SAGILA),
intercede for me!
May he hearken to my cry at the word of thy
mouth!
May he remove my sighing, may he learn my
supplication!
At his mighty word may god and goddess
deal graciously with me!
May the sickness of my body be torn away!
May the groaning of my flesh be consumed!
May the consumption of my muscles be
removed!
May the poisons that are upon me be loosened!
May the ban be torn away may the [...] be
consumed!
May mercy be established among men (and
their) habitations!
May god and king ordain favor
At thy mighty command that is not altered,
and thy true mercy, Oh lady Tašmitu."

* * * * * * *

[*On a tablet describing a lunar eclipse ritual:
after addressing the goddess by name her
suppliant continues.*]

"I ____, son/daughter of ____, whose god is
____, whose goddess is ____,
In the evil of an eclipse of the Moon,
which in ____ a month on ____
a day has taken place
In the evil of the powers, of the portents,
evil and not good, which are in
my palace and my land,
I have turned towards thee!
I have established thee!
Listen to the incantation!
Before Nabu, thy spouse, the lord, the prince,
the first-born son of Isagila (E.SAGILA),
intercede for me!
May he hearken to my cry
at the word of thy mouth;
may he remove my sighing,
may he learn my supplication!
At his mighty word may god and goddess
deal graciously with me!
May the sickness of my body be torn away;
may the groaning of my flesh be consumed!
May the consumption of my muscles be

removed!
May the poisons that are upon me be loosened!
May the ban be torn away, may they be
consumed!
May that with thy command, mercy be
established!
May god and king ordain favor
at thy mighty command that is not altered
And thy true mercy that changes not, O lady
Tašmitu!"

A PRAYER TO SARPANIT
(OLD BABYLONIAN)

"She is mighty, she is divine, she is exalted
among the gods.
Zarpanit, brightest of the stars,
dwelling in *E-ud-ul*.
Shining Beltia, exalted and most high.
Among the goddesses, there is none like her.
She accuses and intercedes.
She abases the rich and vindicates
the cause of the lowly;
She overthrows the enemy,
he who does not revere her godhead;
She delivers the captive,
she takes the hand of the fallen;

Let them tell of thy glory,
let them exalt thy kingdom;
Let them speak of the prowess,
let them glorify thy name;
Have mercy on thy servant who blesses thee.
Take their hand, those in need and suffering
Those in disease and distress, give them life.
May they go forever in joy and delight.
May they tell thy prowess to the people of the
whole world."

PRAYERS TO NABU

"Nabû, prince of heaven and of earth,
who controls harmony [...]
Ninurta, heir to the god Enlil [...]
The one who breaks up mountains [...]
[…] for her (Ištar's) great divinity,
the Sebettu, the supreme gods who,
for the king who reveres them,
they stand at his side,
and make his weapons
prevail over all enemies."

* * * * * * *

"Oh prince, preeminent, first born of Marduk;
Oh prudent ruler, offspring of Sarpanit;

Oh Nabu, bearer of the tablet
of the fate of the gods;
Director of E.SAGILA;
Lord of E.ZIDA, protector of Borsippa;
Beloved of Ea-Enki, granter of life;
Patron of Babylon;
Protector of the living god,
of inhabited hills, of the fortress, of the people;
Lord of temples; thy name is [...]
in the mouth of the people, Oh Shedu!*
Son of the great prince Marduk,
in thy mouth is truth;
in thy illustrious name;
by command of thy great divinity!"

[*The incantation continues for use in healing rites.*]

"I, ____, son/daughter of ____,
who am grievously ill, am thy servant;
whom the hand of the demon
and the poison of [...].
May I live and prosper [...]
Establish (your) truth in my mouth;
Put kindness in my heart.
May the Anunnaki return and be established.
May they proclaim favors to me.
May my god stand at my right hand.

---

* *Sedu* or *si-du*, "*spirit*"—read/spoken as "she-du"

212

May my goddess stand at my left hand.
May the favorable Shedu and
the favorable Lamassu, [...] with me."

* * * * * * *

"O hero, prince, first-born of Marduk
O prudent ruler, offspring of Zarpanitu
O Nabu, Bearer of the tablet of the destiny
of the gods,
Director of Isagila (E.SAGILA)
Lord of Izida (E.ZIDA), Shadow of Borsippa!
Darling of Ia-Enki, Giver of life!
Prince of Babylon, Protector of the living!
God of the hill of dwelling,
the fortress of the nations,
the Lord of temples!
Thy name is in the mouth of the peoples,
O Shedu.
O son of the mighty prince Marduk,
in thy mouth is justice!
In thy illustrious name, at the command
of thy mighty godhead,
I ____, the son/daughter of ____,
who am smitten with disease, thy servant,
Whom the hand of the demon
and the breath of the [...]
May I live, may I be perfect [...]

Set justice in my mouth! [...] mercy in my heart!
May the Anunnaki return and be established!
May they command mercy!
May my god stand at my right hand!
May my goddess stand at my left hand!
May the favorable Shedu,
the favorable Lamassu, (stand) with me!"

[*Directs to make offerings with commencement of
incantation. When used for a healing rite, the sick
person makes a formal statement using their own
name and lineage. The prayer then concludes with
specific requests.*]

"At this time [...] I stand before thee!
Good is thy shadow [...]!
May my way be propitious [...]!
Set a pleasant path for my feet!
O lord, my god, deal graciously with me!
O lord Nabu, my god, deal graciously with me!
In the night season may my dreams be
propitious!
Mercy, compassion, (and) life, O Shedu,
Command, grant my petition and establish me!
At the command of thy mighty godhead
let me live,
let me have knowledge!
In the sight of wide-spread peoples,
may I bow in humility before thee!"

PRAYERS TO MARDUK

"Marduk, great lord, prince,
into whose hand the decrees of
Heaven and Underworld are entrusted.
May the servant who reveres you
be well favored in your presence.
May they have a personal god
and a protecting angel."[†]

* * * * * * *

"Oh, Eternal Ruler,
Lord of everything that exists;
to the king whom thou loves,
and whose name thou last mentioned,
grant that their name may flourish
as seems good to thee.
Guide them on the right path,
I am the prince, thy favorite
creation of thy hand;
Thou created me and entrusted me
rule over everything,
according to thy mercy, O lord,
which thou bestows on all.
Make me to love thy exalted rule.
Cause the fear of divinity
to exist in my heart.

[†]   Kassite *cylinder seal*, c. 1600 BCE.

Grant to me whatever
may seem appropriate to thee
since thou has created my life."

* * * * * * *

"Oh Lord of wisdom, ruler in your own right.
Oh Bel‡, Lord of wisdom, ruler in your own
right.
Oh father Bel, Lord of the lands;
Oh father Bel, Lord of truthful speech;
Oh father Bel, shepherd of the [Babylonians*].
Oh father Bel, who yourself opens the eyes.
Oh father Bel, the warrior, prince among
soldiers;
Oh father Bel, supreme power of the land;
Bull of the corral, warrior who leads
captive all the land.
Oh Bel, proprietor of the broad land;
Lord of creation, you are chief of the land;
The Lord whose shining oil is food
for an extensive offspring.
The Lord whose edicts bind together the city;
The edict of whose dwelling place
strikes down the great prince.
From the land of the rising

---

‡   In Babylon, "*Bel*" is a reference to "*Marduk*."
*   "*Sang-Ngiga*" is the original transliteration.

to the land of the setting sun.
Lord of life, you are indeed Lord!
Oh Bel of the lands, Lord of life,
you, yourself are Lord of life.
Oh mighty one, terrible one of heaven,
you are guardian indeed!
Oh Bel, you are Lord of the gods indeed!
You are father, Bel, who cause the plants
of the gardens to grow!
Oh Bel, your great glory may they fear!
The birds of heaven and the fish of the deep
are filled with fear of you.
Oh father Bel, in great strength you go,
prince of life, shepherd of the stars!
Oh Lord, the secret of production you open,
the feast of fatness establish, to work you call!
Father Bel, faithful prince, mighty prince,
you create the strength of life!"

* * * * * * *

[*The following is self-titled as a "Tablet of Ea-
balassu-iqbi. the son of Bel-apla-iddin, the son of
Nanna-u-tu (. . .) Hand of Marduk-zera-ibni, his
son, the kalu apprentice of Marduk. Babylon, the
10th day of the month (. . .) in Year 178 of the
Seleucid era (when Arsakes was king)."*]

"May the heavens quiet you! May the earth

appease you!
O lord, may the heavens quiet you!
May your beloved spouse, Zarpanitum,
utter a prayer to you!
May the faithful vizier Nabu
utter a prayer to you!
May the daughter-in-law, the first born of Uras
utter a prayer to you!
May the faithful princess Tasmetum
utter a prayer to you!
May the supreme princess, the lady, Nana,
utter a prayer to you!
'You should not reject your city!'
may they say to you!
May they utter a prayer to you!
For how long again?
'You should not reject Babylon!'
May they say to you!
May they utter a prayer to you!
[*uninterpreted lines*]"

A PRAYER TO SAMAS (SHAMMASH)

"O Samas, judge of heaven and earth,
that burns the broad earth!
O Lord, that opens the ear,
the darling of Bil!

Exalted judge,
whose command is not altered;
Whose mercy no god has ever annulled!
A lord art thou, and mighty is thy word!
Thy command is not forgotten,
thy intercession is unequaled
Like Anu, thy father, thy word is exalted!"

PETITIONING THE PANTHEON
(ASSYRIAN / NEO-BABYLONIAN)

"Assur, Marduk.
Nabû, who holds the stylus;
who carries the tablet
of decrees (fates) of the Gods.
Šamaš, the king of heaven and earth;
Sîn, luminous;
Adad, the canal inspector.
Ea-Enki, Lord of wisdom;
who forms all things of every kind,
who fashions creation.
Ištar, Lady of the battle; Ištar my lady;
who loves the king who pleases her,
who subdues (her enemies).
The Sebettu, mighty lords (gods);
who lead my troops;
who strike down my enemies.

219

Amurru, who carries the curved staff
(and) the bucket;
Sumukan, who sets right [...]
The (Anunnaki) great gods;
who dwell in heaven and earth [...]
guard my kingship."

SMALL PRAYERS & BLESSINGS

[*"May the good udug and the good lama stand (as guardians)."*]

udug sa-ga lama sa-ga
he-em-da-su-su-ge-eš

* * * * * * *

[*"Grant that in the mouth of the magician's son thy servant a word may hasten."*]

izib Sa i-na pi mar ambari
ardi-ka ta-mit up-tar-ri-du

* * * * * * *

[*"O Lord, I will sing a song of your divinity."*]

belu luzmur zamar ilutika

* * * * * * *

[*"May Ea-Enki speak for your life."*]

Ea-Enki bala ka liqbi

* * * * * * *

"When you cast the incantation of Eridu,
The evil udug, evil ala, evil ghost, evil galla,
Lamaštu, Laballu, Evil man, evil eye,
evil mouth, evil tongue.
Then they all shall stand aside!
Then the good udug and good lama
shall stand (beside you) as guardians.
Then it shall be adjured by the heavens,
and it shall be adjured by the earth."

A HYMN TO INANNA-ISHTAR

Lady [...]! Returning heroic youth, Inanna [...]
At the shrine, in *Nibiru*,
in the *E.dul.kug* [...] by An,
with the holy crown of An placed on her head,
the most holy *ba* garment of An
draped around her torso,
and the holy scepter of An placed in her hand
—seated on a seat in the assembly,
rendering great judgments in the mountains,
and reaching majestic decisions in all the lands!

Holy Inanna gazes as she shines [...]
down from heaven like a light.

Together with father *Suen* (Nanna-Sin),
the mistress issues commands to the
E.kur.nu.gal of Urim.
In her hands she holds
prosperity for all the lands.
The lady [...] Holy Inanna [...]
[...], you are endowed with beauty [...]

You are she who raises [...] in their prayers.
You are she who displays shining *carnelian*
from the mountains to be admired.
Bringing shinning *lapis lazuli*
from the bright mountain in special baskets,
you are she who, like fire,
melts gold from *Harali*.
You are she who creates apples in their clusters.
You are she who demands [...]
(and) creates the *date* spadices in their beauty.

(*Inanna speaks*)
"When I was living in my dwelling place,
when I was living in An's dwelling,
my lover *Ucumgal-ana* called upon me
to be his wife.
In *Bad-tabira*, from the *E.muc.kalama*,
[...] for his crown."

[...] his assembly, and brought [...] into her holy
shrine for her brother *Ucumgal-ana*.

(*Inanna speaks*)
"[...] stands [...] *Dumuzid* stands in beauty
like an *ildag*-tree.
I will fill my heart with joy.
The one who makes food plentiful [...] on the
bright mound.
My heart is filled with joy,
[...] in heaven and earth.
The house of *Arali* [...]."

[...] the houses in the broad streets [...]
Holy Inanna, your august [...]!
[...] Inanna be praised!

A HYMN TO MARDUK

"Of Běl, mighty hand,
Who lifts up glory and splendor; day of power.
Fearfulness he establishes.
Lord of DUN.PA.UD.DU.A, mighty hand.
The catch-net he throws over the hostile land.
Lord, great warrior, mighty hand.
A firm house he raises up;
the enemy he overthrows.
The shinning one, lord of Nippur, mighty hand.
The lord, the life of the land, the *massŭ*
of heaven and earth."[†]

† *British Musuem.* [K.4980. IV R. 27, No.4]

* * * * * *

"Famed mighty one, chieftain of Eridu;
Exalted prince, first-born of Nudimmud;
Raging Marduk,
restorer of rejoicing to E'engura;
Lord of *E.sag-ila*, hope of Babylon;
Lover of *E.zi-da*, preserver of life;
Lone one of *Emahtilla*, multiplier of the living;
Protector of the land,
savior of the multitudes of people;
The single great one of chapels everywhere,
your name is sweetly hymned by the people
in all places."

A GREAT HYMN TO MARDUK
(ASHURBANIPAL PERSONAL COLLECTION)

I praise your name, Marduk,
the most powerful of the gods,
the canal inspector of heaven and earth [...],
who was well engendered,
and alone is most high [...]!

You bear Anuship, Illilship, Ninŝikuship,
lordship, kingship [...]!
You gather all wisdom, total strength [...]!

Honored ruler, exalted monarch,

overpowering, magnificent [...]!
They glorified his lordship,
prepared battle, [...] Anu!

You are exalted in the heavens, king on earth,
the skillful counselor of the great gods [...],
establisher of all habitations,
grasper of the discs of the celestial firmament
and all the lands!

You are magnificent among the gods,
Nudimmud beautified your features [...];
the great gods made you hold fast in your hand
the tablet of destinies and gave you the power
to raise and lower; they kissed your feet
and proclaimed, blessing you:
"He alone is king!"

To [...] the enemies, Illil made magnificent
for you the decrees [...]!
Great [...] of the gods, bright radiance,
[...] sheen, [...] who goes about
amidst the heavens [...]!
[...] smiter of the skull of Anzū,
defeater of [...], [...], the mad dog,
the bison, the fish-man [...];
[...] divided them [...]

Heir of Nudimmud, [...] your eyes [...]

You [...] a bow, merciless arrows,
swords, weapons of war [...]
You vanquished broad Tiamat,
[...] Qingu, her spouse.

May Babylon exult in you and
E.sagila rejoice over you,
wherein you pass just and rightful judgment,
decide the decisions for [...],
let loose water from the underground sources,
cause copious rains, raise huge floods.

The greatness of Bel, canal inspector of heaven,
is truly great,
he is much mightier than the gods, his fathers!
He excels in form, is most high in stature,
magnificent in his lordly apparel.

He summoned the Igigi and the Anunnaki,
they kneel before him, and the gods who begot
him repose in silence at his feet.
To take advice, to consult in lordly consultation,
their attention is directed
towards Marduk alone.

Offerings, incense, censers,
stringed inu-instruments, harps and [...]
are set out; they glorify the builder of E.sagila,
Babylon rejoices, [...] is exuberant!

The *Igigi*, *Anunnaki*, the gods and goddesses
of cult centers, shrines and daises submit to you!
The governors and advisers
pray to your majesty.

Eldest son of Nudimmud,
primordial, brave, strong, the merciless storm,
raging fire, scorching flame burning the enemy,
who in the midst of battle does not fear the clash
of weapons and engagement in combat.

The most lofty in stature,
Marduk, the flaring sun,
light-giving lantern, who in his magnificence
[...], who purifies the unclean,
and makes the [...] to shine.

May all the gods and every goddess,
Anu, Illil-Enlil, the constellations, the Abyss,
the solid ground, Nudimmud along with the
[...] Lahmu gods, Cancer and Pisces,
witness the deeds of the lord of the gods,
Marduk and may they constantly
[...] everlasting [...].

Forever present me with the *bursag*-offerings,
pure [...], [...] which the irascible* god [...]
by his exalted command established to give

---

* *"Irascible"* — easily angered.

vigor to those endowed with life.

Your shining name is Jupiter,
the first-ranking god,
the foremost of the foremost,
the highest god, who [...], who at his rising
makes manifest a sign, [...] the Pleiades [...].

Noble, magnificent, Egišgalanna,
the lord who [...] the celestial positions
of the *Anunnaki*, who [...] purification rites,
rituals, and offerings [...].

Your utterance is most great,
Marduk, raging [...]!
You are the greatest among all the gods,
your divinity [...] the gods [...].

Prince, praiseworthy, shrouded one!
In your net [...]; on your right is [...],
on your left is Erragal,
the strongest one of the gods,
in front of you go the valiant Pleiades!
Fire burns to the right and left [...],
wherever you have raged.

Most honored, most splendid
—how splendid he is, the god to whom [...]
subject themselves, [...] his divinity!

To all the gods who occupy daises,
he munificently endows food
and cereal offerings [...].

Marduk made firm and grasped in his hand
the lead ropes of the *Igigi* and *Anunnaki*,
the mainstay of Heaven and the Underworld.
In the east and west he set up constellations,
gave them roads and passages [...].

Judge of the four regions
is your weighty sworn name,
the circumspect one, Illil-Enlil of the great gods,
who establishes the rules of the Abyss,
gives allotments and food offerings
to the great gods.

Receive my supplications,
accept my humble entreaties, [...];
may the god who pleases you
constantly speak favorably to you of me!

May Anu, Illil-Enlil, Ea-Enki,
make your mood jubilant
and your heart exuberant!
May Damkina, your great mother,
command you to be at peace in *E.sagila*,
the place which you love.

She is venerable, queenly, strong;
she is mistress, spouse, goddess, lady,
proud, great, lofty, beautiful, Zarpanit!
Great lady, beloved consort of Marduk;
O beloved mother of Nabu-Tutu,
let me live and I will sing your praises!

Let me glorify your mighty deeds,
O majestic princess, queen of *Esagila*,
goddess of goddesses, queen of queens,
elevated queen of all [...],
merciful goddess who loves prayers!

I pray to you, proud, raging loud:
May your angered heart find rest,
may your enraged mind relent and be appeased!
May I find life in your breath,
lofty sage of the gods, Marduk!

⚜ 6 ⚜
RITES, RITUALS & CEREMONIES

"I am the priestess of Marduk and Sarpanit.
I am the daughter of E.ri-du
and the high priestess in Babylon.
I am the priestess of Nabu and Teshmet.
I am the daughter of E.zi-da
and the high priestess in Borsippa."

<u>INITIATION & ORDINATION</u>

Initiation to the "inner-circle" priesthood of ancient Mesopotamia was far more exclusive than
what we would find in modern practices today. Of
course, not all members of the priesthood required
such an initiation to hold their office. For example,
the 'unconsecrated lamentation hymnists' (*kalû la
gul-lu-bu*) and 'diviners' (*baru*) could operate as
clergy without achieving high-level initiation.
However, only true initiates were permitted to
enter the "inner sanctum" of the Temple and/or attend to needs of the gods.

It was the responsibility of high ranking priestesses and priests to choose their own successors
and guarantee perpetual continuity of the Mardukite cult. But these selections had to be
approved. An individual candidate (or their spon-
sor) had to formally petition the Temple with a

written application. In all cases, the procedure leading to a priesthood initiation began with a formal written request addressed to the *šatammu*—the highest administrative authority of cult affairs (at the local level).

Upon receipt of an application, the Temple-courts (*šatammu*) began their preliminary investigation of the candidate. But, officially consecrating new clergy was also a state affair. Therefore, royal permission had to be obtained. The Temple and Palace cooperated in handling all civil affairs. Certain clergy held specialized offices in the Palace and frequently accompanied the King (and court) in their endeavors. The *šatammu* expertly protected the regulations and interests of the Temple; yet, officially, the King still retained the final word regarding new clergy, internal promotions, and removing administrative staff.

Becoming an "ordained" (officially recognized) priestess or priest did not happen all at once. Often, the process unfolded in three stages. In the first stage, divination is employed to select an interested candidate—and therefore demonstrating by some oracular means that they are truly "chosen" for this role (by divine ordinance) —"separate from the profane/mundane world." Secondly, the "novitiate" had to learn more details about the religious tradition and its rituals—much like what you find in this book. The final step is to actually "incorporate the individual into the spiritual world" via formal initiation and vocational practice.

The actual initiation ceremony begins with preparation of the candidate with an elaborate *'Purification Rite'* [see next section] prior to ever entering the inner Temple for the the first time. Any attending priestesses, priests and officiates, had to be clean and oil-anointed (as per their own standard rite) before entering the Temple as well. Formal initiation (or ordination) into Babylon's "secret society" carried three additional qualifications or requirements, which were tested (or attested to) during the rite: *purity of body, purity of blood,* and *purity of mind.*

The first qualification for initiation was *'purity of the body'.* [Refer also to *'Purification Rite'* section that follows.] But this included elements that one had little normal control over. For example, one could not suffer from poor eyesight, kidney-stones, or even bare an asymmetrical face. They were to be as "pure as a golden statue"—a perfect "outward" portrayal or reflection of the "divinity" represented.

The second requirement was to be of the right family (genetic) descent. This is perhaps the first time in history we find a reference to a *'purity of blood'.* This was verified by checking on one's parental lineage. [This also means that two of three qualifications were beyond one's ability to change.] We cannot be certain exactly what standards were followed—but we might assume that an individual could not publicly/politically represent a deity if they notoriously came from a scandalous or criminal family.

The third and final check was mental in nature--'*purity of mind*'. By this, we of course mean a test of mental fortitude, emotional clarity, and the ability to retain adequate vocational training. Some might argue that a candidate had to prove aptitude or intelligence; but most of what was necessary could be learned or developed (if one were able and willing). Thereafter, formal tests of one's "cultic suitability" continued to occur regularly throughout one's vocational career.

Apart from the notes detailing the '*Purification Rite*', we cannot be absolutely certain what kind of actions or rhetoric is applied to this over-night '*Initiation*' process. However, at the end of the ceremony, the initiate emerges from their experience as the sun dawns. They speak:

"At dawn my hands are washed.
May a propitious beginning start for me.
May happiness and good health
ever accompany me.
Whatsoever I seek, may I attain it.

May the dream I dreamed
be made favorable for me.
May anything evil, anything unfavorable;
The spittle of warlock and witch,
not reach me, not touch me;
By the command of EA-Enki, Šamaš,
Marduk, and the princess Bēlet-ilī."

'PURIFICATION RITE' (NOTES)

"Not only perfect of body, but perfect of mind;
When one becomes pure, they become god-like;
They become acceptable servants of the gods."

Only clergy "prefects" (ex: *erib-biti, nešakku, pašišu, &tc.*) were allowed to enter the innermost sanctums of the Temple, or given the task of *qurrubu sa naptani*—the privilege of bringing food to, caring for, or otherwise being at all near, the gods themselves. All high-level priestesses and priests were required to follow a strict regimen or self-care (regarding hygiene and appearances).

All clergy were required to maintain themselves all the time, but were required to cleanse and purify immediately before entering the sacred areas of the Temple. However, the day of their initiation would have been the first time that an individual was subjected to these higher standards. Hence the

'*Purification Rite*' (or *gullubu*; "ritual shaving") attached to the '*Initiation*' is a much lengthier "cosmetic make-over" process than one would normally require to simply maintain it thereafter.

The '*purification*' segment took place during the day; the '*initiation*', at night (and lasting until the following dawn). The candidate is prepared with the '*purification rite*' in a private bath-house (within the Temple District) before they are permitted to enter the actual Temple for the '*initiation*'. The '*rite*' begins with a full physical examination (by the *ašipu*, or physician-priest). Determining that there are no physical blemishes, disfigurements, poor eyesight, chipped teeth, damaged hands, or skin disease, and so forth, the candidate is ready to proceed with their ritual purification.

During the ritual, an *ašipu* recites a repetitive series of (sixteen) incantation-prayers over the candidate while they are completely shaven (*gullubu*), washed /cleansed (*ramku*), and their nails are trimmed. [Priestesses were permitted long-hair; but it was separated into two braided parts or *plaits*, with their lengths wrapped across and secured/pinned over the crown of the head—known today as the '*heidi*'/*milkmaid* braid '*up do*'.] This clean-cut appearance distinguished high-ranking members of the priesthood from the otherwise mundane animal-like appearance of common humans.

During the course of this day-long event, the candidate was not permitted to eat meat and could only drink water. Toward the end, they are anointed with oil and their mouth is washed. They are given the *kubsu* (bleached white wool turban of their office). And after all of this, they are finally ready for service of the highest order—ready to present themselves (and speak) to a god!

'PRIESTESS INSTALLATION' (NOTES)

"The (high priestess) of EA-Enki am I.
The (high priestess) of Damkina am I.
The messenger of Marduk am I.
My spell is the spell of EA-Enki.
My incantation is the incantation of Marduk.
The circle of EA-Enki is in my hand.
The tamarisk, the powerful weapon of Anu;
In my hand I hold,
The date-spathe, mighty in decision;
In my hand I hold."

Ceremonial '*installation*' of a priestess is treated very similar to an elaborate wedding—and it marked a sacred marriage between the initiate and the divine. On the *first* day, a girl is selected from the elite by divination (presumably 'drawing lots'). She is anointed and purified at her father's house. On day *two*, there is a procession to the Temple of their deity. Her hair is cut and she is anointed in the courtyard before returning home. The *third* day requires making personal offerings to the deity, which must be "accepted" in order for an '*installation*' (*malluku*) to be approved. On the *fourth* day there is a procession to various holy shrines, including more offerings, and finally, a banquet.

During the '*installation*' she received golden rings and bracelets, serving as her own personal '*dowry*' from the gods—given directly to (and owned by) the priestess (unlike in traditional marriages). She is given a red-dyed wool headdress bearing an insignia appropriate to her office/role within the priesthood. On days *five* to *eleven*, a local seven-day celebration occurred in the Temple District. On the (final) *eleventh* day, she was dressed in bleached-white garments of a bride. She is carried in procession by her 'brothers'; her 'sister' washes her feet. She is given a bedchamber with a chair or footstool by the elders. She gracefully descends up the bed, lying in wait for arrival of the deity...

PREPARATORY OPENING RITES
(TABLET FRAGMENTS)

"Do the following.[†]
Before Marduk, set a SA.NA of incense,

---

† *Siptu bit nu-ru* ritual tablet.

a SA of oil, a drink-offering, water;
Honey (and) butter shalt thou offer,
[...] the seed of the *mastakal*-plant;
in the middle of the oil cast [...];
recite the incantation and anoint with oil."

[Similar instructions from another tablet source.]

"Pure water shalt thou sprinkle.
The [...] drink-offering shalt thou present.
Dates and [...] shalt thou heap up.
[...] oil and drink-offering, water,
honey (and) butter shalt thou offer.
An incense-burner shalt thou set there.
The [...]-drink shalt thou pour out."

INCANTATION OF ERIDU (THE DEEP)
(MARDUKITE GRAND INVOCATION)[*]

"Anu, above me, King in Heaven.
Enlil, Commander of the Airs.
Enki, Lord of the Deep Earth.
I am Nabu; hear my words.
I am the priest(ess) of Marduk and Sarpanit.
Born of EA-Enki and Damkina.

---

[*] *Tablet-W* translation in *"The Complete Anunnaki Bible"*; originally derived from *"The Complete Book of Marduk by Nabu"* (*Liber-W*).

I am the priest(ess) in E.ri.du.

I am the magician in Babylon.

My spell is the spell of Ea-Enki.

My incantation is the incantation of Marduk.

The Tablets of Destiny, I hold in my hands.

The [Sign]‡ of Anu and Antu,

I hold in my hands.

The wisdom of Enlil and Ninlil, I call to me.

The Magic Circle of EA-Enki and Damkina,

I conjure about me.

Shammash and Aya are before me.

Nanna-Sin and Ningal are behind me.

Nergal and Ereshkigal are at my right side.

Ninurta and Ba'u are at my left side.

Blessed light of Ishtar and Dumuzi shines

favorably upon my sacred work.

It is not I, but Marduk,

who performs the incantations."

THE ASHIPU RITUALIST (TRAINING)
(EXORCISM RITES & SPIRITUAL HEALING)

The two primary means of expelling evil spirits are *water* and *fire*. These two elements can cleanse

---

‡ This word is translated to mean "*tamarisk*," "*scepter*," or "*ankh*" (or "*rod and ring*") in different versions.

everything from "evil"—even entire worlds. So, when gods are called upon, they are the gods of *water* and *light*. One might note, from previous reading in this present book, that *water* is the essential foundation of most religious ceremonies (and magical rites) in Babylon—but especially those concerned with the removal of "*evil spirits.*" All other means utilized toward this purpose were subordinate to *water.* Above all, *spring-water* was most sacred; many temples even maintained their own springs.

The *maqlu* series or "*burning*" rites—purification by *fire*—are treated in a separate volume in this series. Those tablets pertain to countering "magic spells" of evil witches and warlocks operating against the well-being of the community (or civilization) as a whole. In this section, we will treat the *siptu* incantation-tablets, or "spiritual exorcisms" that banish "evil spirits" (from the body) with blessed *water.*

Mesopotamian knowledge of "magic" and "religion"—which is also to say, science and medicine—originated with the prehistoric cult in Eridu, dedicated to EA-Enki (not surprisingly, the Anunnaki god of *water*). In ancient times, the city of Eridu was located near the mouth of the Euphrates and Tigris rivers, directly on the shores of the *abzu*, or *apsu*, or "the Deep"—the "Persian Gulf"—which the Babylonians perceived as a direct connection between *this* material world and the *Celestial Abzu.*

Cuneiform tablets often read like brief narratives when offering "magical" (or "medicinal") wisdom. In many cases, a '*younger god*' will go and appeal to an '*elder god*' for advice on a specific matter. Within the context of the dialogue, some prescription or instruction will be found. Such tablets were collected in libraries and used as references for treating present issues. [The "*omen tablets*" are also based on past observations of synchronicity, which are then later referred to for advice when similar conditions occur again—a practice Babylonians eventually standardized as "*astrology.*"]

For a most basic example (on one tablet citing a narrative from Eridu): EA-Enki is revered as the God of Absu; Marduk as a young Lord of the Springs. Marduk asks for advice on healing the "sick man." EA-Enki directs him to take water from the mouth of the two rivers (the Tigris and Euphrates) and sprinkle it on the "sick man." The direction to "perform the incantation" led to the basic practice of a priest(ess) sprinkling a sick (or unclean, impure) individual with water while reciting a prayer.

"*When one has become sick, they are under the influence of grievous spirits.*" As primitive as that belief may seem to a modern reader, it does not really propose anything different than "*germ theory*." The truth is that while physical symptoms may be recessed in a person, modern ("western") medicine does not have a clear understanding on the underlying nature of disease—particularly where it concerns other living organisms acting upon the body. That living cells or viruses may have their own center of consciousness or a "spiritual awareness" (and therefore intelligence or even intentional third-party programming) is barely even considered when treating and handling such things today.[†] ["Evil spirits" were also thought to hide in dark corners, stale dusty environments, and even ritual objects—which is why the tools and sacred spaces are always purified before any magical/religious ritual/ceremonial work is conducted.]

In Babylon, the "sick person" prays with (and through) the *asipu* (*ashipu*) or *mas.masu* (*mashmashu*) to be freed from "evil" that has come into his body. The priest(ess) then sprinkles them with blessed "holy water" (*mū ellu*) while reciting a *siptu*-exorcism to expel the "evil spirits." If they "win" this "spiritual battle" against the spirit, then

---

[†] Refer to either "*Entities and Fragments: Systemology Advanced Training Course Manual #5*," "*Keys to the Kingdom (Volume 2)*" or "*The Complete Keys to the Kingdom (Workbook Edition)*" by Joshua Free.

health is renewed; but if they "fail" there will be "death" (or unconsciousness)—they journey to the "*underworld*" (or else the domain of "evil spirits") for an indeterminate period of time until being sprinkled by the gods (there) with the '*waters of life*'.

The "magical force" or "spiritual authority" of the *siptu*-incantation is tied to vocalization of the god-names. Babylonians attached "power" to *divine names*—something which continued thereafter in most cultures and spiritual traditions. ['*Kabbalistic*' and '*hermetic*' traditions inherited the knowledge directly from Babylon.] The "power" of the deity was believed to be connected (in some way) to their various titles and names —each carrying a very specific meaning. The literal frequency-vibration (or sound) and cuneiform appearance of these titles was of such importance that *divine names* from the older Sumerian language were also retained (for their "power") in Babylonian tradition.

A *siptu*-incantation may be spoken once; but more often it was recited three times for a stronger effect. Its context is similar to what is found with more modern "exorcisms" today—such as the verbiage used by the Catholic Church—*e.g.* "*The power of Christ compels you,*" "*In Jesus' name...*" *&tc.* A few tablet-fragments are included below as examples of basic formulae. It is not uncommon to end the incantation with a simple roll-call of *names* and *titles* of the various gods invoked within the prayer. But, perhaps of all the possible lines that can be included, the most paramount is usually the most direct:

NĪŠ IL ___ LŪ TAMĀTU

or

NĪŠ IL ___ UTAMMËKA

"In the name of ___, I exorcise thee."

* * * * * * *

EXAMPLE 1
(long formula)

"In the name of Heaven, be thou exorcised!
In the name of Earth, be thou exorcised!
In the name of Bel, lord of the world,
be thou exorcised!
In the name of Beltis, mistress of the world,
be thou exorcised!
In the name of Ninib, mighty warrior of Bel,
be thou exorcised!
In the name of Nuzku,
the exalted messenger of Bel,
be thou exorcised!
In the name of Istar, mistress of mankind,
be thou exorcised!
In the name of Adad.

the lord whose thunder is good,
be thou exorcised!
In the name of Samas, lord of judgment,
be thou exorcised!
In the name of the Anunnaki, the great gods,
be thou exorcised!"

* * * * * * *

EXAMPLE 2
(usual formula)

In the name of Heaven, be thou exorcised!
In the name of Earth, be thou exorcised!

* * * * * * *

EXAMPLE 3
(simple)

In the name of the great gods, be thou exorcised!

* * * * * * *

EXAMPLE 4

I exorcise thee by Anu, father of the great gods!

* * * * * * *

EXAMPLE 5

In the name of the Anunnaki, I exorcise thee!

That thou are commanded to depart.

* * * * * * *

EXAMPLE 6
(*siptu closing*)

In the name of Heaven, be thou exorcised!
In the name of Earth, be thou exorcised!
Šedu (*shedu*); Lama—Lamma—Lammasu!

AN EXAMPLE EXORCISM TABLET
(BABYLONIAN)

"Marduk, the son of E.ri-du,
placed his hand upon him;
He performed the incantation:
Bring a censer and a torch (and say)
'May the plague demon Namtar,
who is in the body of this person,
trickle away like water.'
Take the copper of might of the hero Anu,
which by the roar of its splendor
removes the evil (and say)
'An evil demon art thou;
a god who walks in the night;
whose unclean hands
do not know reverence.
An evil demon art thou

who lies down in wait for the man,
resting like an ass.
An evil demon art thou;
who knows not sacrifice,
and who has no gifts.
Disease is all you know;
snare and burden is all you have.
But in mercy, the god gladly
vindicates good for him,
unto Shamash [...]'."

REASONS FOR HEADACHES, DISEASES AND POSSESSION
('SURPU' DIAGNOSTIC-LIST TABLET)[†]

The person who has...

...sinned against their God

...sinned against their Goddess.

...misconducted themselves before the God.

...misconducted themselves before the Goddess.

...made their God and Goddess angry with them.

...sought undue secrets of the Gods of Heaven.

...sought undue secrets of the Temple-Shrines of Earth.

[†]   Excerpt from *Mardukite Tablet-H* series; reprinted in "*The Complete Anunnaki Bible*."

...slighted what is due to the Gods.

...sought undue favor of the Gods at the Temple-Shrines.

...offered impure sacrifice at the Altar of Offering.

...offered sacrifice [*to the Gods*] and taken it back.

...destroyed the sacrifice made at the Altar of Offering.

...obstructed the sacrifices made by another.

...caused obstruction between [*friends or family*].

...eaten flesh of a sacrifice at the Altars of Offering.

...held hatred towards an elder.

...shed his neighbor's blood.

...propositioned their neighbor's wife.

...propositioned their neighbor's husband.

...used a false balance in business affairs.

...removed or misplaced a boundary or landmark.

...unjustly entered their neighbor's house.

...taken their neighbor's garment.

...stolen or caused another to steal.

...said "no" for "yes" and "yes" for "no." [*lying*]

...been straight in the mouth but not true in the heart.

...promised pleasure and joy but not given it.

...spoken of what is unholy.

...spoken wickedness.

...caused a judge to receive a bribe.

...wronged their city.

...opposed one in authority under Marduk.

...give in small things but refused in great.

...transgressed the righteous.

...offended the righteous.

...set their hand to evil acts.

...set their hearts to follow after evil.

...stopped a neighbor's canal. [*water supply*]

...been banned of weapons but seeks them.

...set their hand to evil sorceries and witchcraft.

...pointed at the holy fire.

...taken a prolonged seat in the sun. [*sun-stroke*]

...struck the young of an animal.

...tearing up plants in the desert.

...tearing of plants and trees.

...raised a fire and falsely sworn by a god.

...has tasted from the unclean cup.

...has tasted from the unclean plate.

...has tasted from the unclean dish.

...performed an unknown sin against their God.

...performed an unknown sin against their Goddess.

THE ASHIPU 'GHOST RITE'
(ARCHAIC EXAMPLE)

"Šamaš, king of Heaven and Earth;
Šamaš, judge of the lands;
Šamaš, foremost of the gods;
Šamaš, mighty and resplendent one;
Šamaš, lord who makes things go aright."

Based on descriptions given on tablets, we can interpret "ghost-pains" or "phantom pains" as those which are not connected to an (visible) injury or illness—such as a painful "stinging" sensation, &tc. Mesopotamians believed that "demons" and their diseases (or apparent 'side-effects') could be caught using knots, bands, threads, strings, and amulets (tied around the affected area). In many regards, the same "religio-magical" principles apply to handling "ghost-pains."

To provide an example: one tablet provides instructions for a ritual procedure (to combat "ghost-pains") that directs the priest(ess) to scatter *burašu*-juniper on *ašagū*-thorn charcoal in a censer before (an image of) Shammash. Then beer is offered in libation. Some hair from a virgin she-goat and some hair from a virgin lamb are twined together into a *cord*. Then *three knots* are tied *seven times*.* Whenever one is tied, the (above) incan-

---

* The ambiguous writing is unclear whether 3-x-7,

tation is recited three times before (the image of) Shammash. Then the *knotted-cord amulet* is tied onto the patient wherever they feel the stinging. If the condition doesn't subside within a month, the process is repeated (where the knots are loosened and then tied again).

THE ASHIPU 'PASASU RITE'
(ARCHAIC EXAMPLE)

Pasasu is the '*Rite of Anointing*'—which is referenced in virtually every ritual text and ceremony (and throughout this book) wherever "oil" and/or "anointing" is mentioned. This practice was so paramount to the religio-magical (and medical) tradition that the terms *pasisu* and *asipu* became virtually synonymous. An anointing rite may be applied by a priest(ess): to themselves; to each other (clergy); to common citizens; to idols/statuary (and other religious tools/implements); and to a home (or any space consecrated for ritual purposes).

While *olive oil* or *palm oil* served as the most common base, other substances and oils might be mixed with it—either according to some special "secret" recipe, or as indicated on instruction-tablets. The most common additives were raw herbs

---

or *21* individual knots, are tied along its length— or if the same three knots are loosened and retied.

and essential oils, such as: myrtle, myrrh, frankincense, cedar, marjoram, hyssop, coriander and cinnamon. *Note that essential oils are not for internal consumption.*

The following is a standard example of the '*Rite of Anointing*', which begins with a preliminary invocation. It is unclear whether this first incantation is used while the *anointing-oil* is being prepared, *or* prior to entering the house (as this is describing an *asipu* house-call), *or* both.

> "Ea-Enki, King of the Deep,
> I, the magician, am thy slave.
> March thou on my right hand;
> Assist me on my left.
> Add thy pure spell to mine;
> Add thy pure voice to mine.
> Vouchsafe (to me) pure words.
> Make fortunate the utterances of my mouth.
> Ordain that my decisions be happy,
> Let me be blessed wherever I tread.
> Let the man whom I now touch be blessed,
> Before me may lucky thoughts be spoken,
> After me may a lucky finger be pointed.
> Thou are my guardian genius,
> And my guardian spirit!
> Oh, Marduk, the god that blesses.
> Let me be blessed, wherever my path may be!

Thy power, shall god and man proclaim;
    This [...] shall do thy service,
    And I too, the magician, thy slave."

* * * * * * *

[*Incantation, upon entering the house...*]

"Shammash (is) before me,
    Nanna-Sin (is) behind me,
    Nergal (is) at my right hand,
    Ninib-Ninurta (is) at my left hand.
When I draw near unto the sick one;
When I lay my hand on the head of the sick one;
May a kindly Spirit, a kindly Guardian,
    stand at my side."

* * * * * * *

[*Incantation, for each time the oil is applied.*]

"Pure oil, clean oil, bright oil,
    Oil that brings abundance to the gods,
    Oil that eases the sinews of men,
    Oil of the exorcism of Ea-Enki,
    Oil of the exorcism of Marduk;
I have made thee abundant with oil of easing,
    Which Ea-Enki has given for easing;
    I have anointed thee with the oil of life;
I have pronounced the exorcism of Ea-Enki,

the lord of Eridu, and Nin-[...];
I have expelled the *asakku*, the *ahhazu*,
The trembling of thy body;
I have driven out the cry of pain
and anguish of thy body,
I have eased the sinews of thy afflicted limbs;
By command of Ea-Enki, king of the deep,
By the spell of Ea-Enki,
And By the conjuration of Marduk;
By the binding of the of [...]-la,
By the two easing hands of Nin-[...];
Of Ninahakuddu, mistress of the
holy-water-bowl;
___ the son/daughter of ___ is restored to life
[...], Ea-Enki, exorcism [...]
[...] of Eridu may ease the body [...]"

'BEDCHAMBER RITES' (NOTES)
(SACRED MARRIAGE)

*"Carry the ceremonial bed down the river,
to the sacred Temple of Aššur.
As long as the bed is aboard,
watch over it day and night;
and make regular offerings in front of it."*

The most complete surviving Mesopotamian records of a *'sacred marriage'* reenactment (*'love*

ritual or *quršu*) involving actual '*copulation*' ('*coitus*', or *garašu*) are Assyrian (or at best, for our purposes, from the Neo-Assyrian Babylonian Renaissance era). Other than "healing rites" (involving a '*sick bed*'), the '*love ritual*' is practically the only time a '*bed*' (*eršu*) is referenced on religio-magical tablets. In this case, a specific '*ceremonial bedchamber*' (*bet erši*) provides the setting.

Assyrian tablets refer to an elaborate week-long '*love ritual*' celebrated in *Assur*-city (at the '*Temple of Aššur*') each year during the eleventh month (*Shebat*). The '*bet erši*' became a major part of royal festivities during the reign of King Assurbanipal, after the reconstruction of *Ešarra*. Letters written by religious officials at the '*Temple of Nabû*' in *Calah*-city suggest a similar annual rite (dedicated specifically to Nabû and Tašmetu) took place there in the beginning of the second month (*Iyyar*).

LOVE RITUAL OF NABU & TESHMET

"Tašmetu, the Great Lady,
your beloved spouse who intercedes for me daily,
is before you in the sweet bed;
who never ceases demanding
that you protect my life.
Oh Nabû, the one who trusts in you
will not come to shame."

Aside from the romantic epics and cult-literature dedicated to Inanna-Ishtar and Dumuzi (Tammuz), *"The Love Ritual of Nabû and Tašmetu"* is perhaps the best documented Anunnaki 'sacred marriage' (and more appropriate for *Mardukite Babylonian* tradition). Our primary source for this information comes from discourse (correspondence letters) exchanged among 'temple administrators' (*hazannu*) and kings. We have collected some of the best preserved examples below. Some details differ between accounts, mainly regarding which day a thing happens. It is also possible that the version used in Assyria was different from the version in Babylon (as described by Mardukite *priest-king*, Nabû-šumu-iddina, *c.* 880 BCE).

The *"Nabû and Tašmetu Quršu Festival"* takes place during the first 11-12 days of the second month, *Iyyar* (or *Airu*). Presumably, all preparations are completed on the first day of the month (*1-Iyyar*) because the tablets indicate that the first day of the actual ritual is *2-Iyyar*. That day (*2-Iyyar*) is approximately April 22nd. This is one month after the *Akiti* "New Year" is celebrated on March 21st when the *"Sun entered Aries"* (*1-Nissanu*).

What the Mesopotamian *Quršu* provides us with, is a Mardukite parallel tradition to the European-pagan *"Beltane"* (literally, *'Fires of Bel'*) fertility festival—which coincides with the '*May-flower blossoming'* (approximately April 20 – May 1). Astronomically, both of these annual festivals—*Beltane* and *Quršu*—began when the *"Sun entered Taurus."* The religio-magical purpose behind these "love rituals" or "sacred marriage ceremonies" is the bestowal of fertility and divine blessing upon the land and its people.

On the *first* day of the festival-ritual (*2-Iyyar*), a fresh *erši*-bed (apparently freighted to the site via the river) is carried to the inner temple—to the sacred "bedchamber" (*bet erši*) or "nuptial chamber" (*hammutu*). The chamber is "prepared for the erotic rendezvous of Nabû and Tašmetu." All of the "wedding guests"—the attending 'gods' (or at least their 'statues')—arrive at the Temple on the second festival day (*3-Iyyar*).

Ša 4 Ajjaru Nabû Tašmetum ina bet erši errubu
"On the 4th day of Iyyar,
Nabû and Tašmetu will enter the bed chamber."

ana badi Nabû Tašmetum ina bet erši errubu
"Tomorrow (on the 4th day), in the evening,
Nabû and Tašmetu will enter the bed chamber."

Some versions suggest that Nabû enters the bedchamber alone on the third festival day (*4-Iyyar*) and that Tašmetu arrives on the fourth day for the "wedding night" and "intercourse" (start of the 'honeymoon'). Others say that Nabû and Tašmetu entered the bedchamber together on the fourth festival day (5-*Iyyar*). Whichever day they do travel the streets to enter the bedchamber, it is marked by a grand public procession to the Temple—Tašmetu emerging from her '*holy workshop*' (*mummu*) and Nabû from his '*tablet house*' (*bet tuppi*). Praises and hymns are sung and chanted, inviting the "divine couple" to "come and enter the bedchamber."

The tablets ambiguously direct for the "wedding feast" (*šakussu ša šarri*) to occur on either the fifth ritual day or the fifth day of *Iyyar* (which is the fourth ritual day); after which the couple stayed in the bedchamber for five (or six) days before emerging again. For the duration of their intimate rendezvous, they are nourished by repeated bedside '*Rites of Offering*' performed only by the highest temple administrators. Food for the wedding feast, and other offerings and gifts, are donated by the royal family and other high ranking members of the community—but really, all citizens were invited to participate. The correlating instructions from Nabû-šumu-iddina's correspondence continue:

> *niqiatišunu u[bbalina] pan Nabû Tašme[tum]*
> *ina bet er[ši] eppaš*
> "I will bring the offerings before Nabû and Tašmetu,
> and will perform the rites in the bedroom."

šakussu ša šarri ušakkulu hazannu uššab
"On the 5th day, they will serve the royal banquet.
The administrator will attend."

hazannu ša bet Nabû anaku lallik [ina] Kalhi
"I am the administrator of the temple of Nabû.
I should therefore go to Calah"

šamallû ša niqîšu ibaššuni eppaš ša 1 qa
aklišu ušella ina bet Nabû ekkal
"Of the apprentice priests,
whoever has a sacrifice
to make will do so;
and whoever brings even one
bit of food may eat it in the Temple of Nabû."

issu libbi UD.5.KAM adi UD.10.KAM [il]ani ina
bet erši šunu u hazannu [k]ammus
"From the 5th to the 10th, the gods will be in
the bed chamber; the administrator will sit by."

From the 5th until the 10th day, Nabû and Tašmetu stay in the bedchamber (with the temple administrator in their presence). The tablets make obvious implications that intimate relations occur for the duration. The goddess Tašmetu, while gratifying her beloved in the '*sweet bed*', makes appeals to him based on the king's petitions (made on behalf of the greater community of citizens/worshipers).

The insinuation here is that Nabû is most receptive to the requests when he is properly 'appeased'.

On the 11th day, Nabû emerges from the bedchamber to "stretch his legs" with a walk through the royal gardens. A chariot transports him through the city—and this post-wedding procession from the Temple through the city (which ends with his returning the *tablet house*') is the final phase of the festival-ritual. There final details regarding Tašmetu (from this point) do not appear on any surviving examples. We are perhaps led to assume that she remains in the bedchamber on the final day, 'resting' from her week of 'activity'.

A DIVINE MENAGE-A-TROIS

Obscure Mardukite tablet records and a recovered *kudurru* text allude to the god Nabu sharing a "sacred marriage" with two different goddesses— Nanaya and Tašmetu—forming a divine '*love triangle*'. This is unique for the Mardukite lineage, which mainly consisted of Marduk and Nabu; but it was a common practice in the older Anunnaki pantheon. Male deities would typically have both an "official" and an "unofficial" female consort in order to beget two distinct bloodlines. [Anunnaki "half-siblings" (by the same father) could be betrothed to each other *only if* they were born from different mothers.]

Fragments of an 'Old-Babylonian' (Akkadian) era love-poem/narrative, dated to approximately 1700 BCE, define Nanaya and Mu'ati—a variant name for Nabu—as a divine couple. This would, in fact, predate the "sacred marriage" between Nabû and Tašmetu that is strongly emphasized a thousand years later during the 'Neo-Assyrian' (Babylonian Renaissance) period. Nanaya and Tašmetu definitively maintained separate residences in Babylon; so we know the two aren't different names for the same persona. It is quite possible that Nanaya was Nabu's original consort during the Sumerian (Enlilite) era, when their Amorite/Amurru/Martu (pre-Babylonian Mardukite) cult still confined itself west of Mesopotamia and in Egypt.

'Old-Babylonian' era Mardukites celebrated a 'love-ritual' (hadašš utu) for Nabû and Nanaya that parallels the "Nabû and Tašmetu Quršu Festival" observed during the 'Babylonian Renaissance'. That the two are so similar is of benefit to us, since we have far fewer details for the older one. They both were celebrated in the second month (Iyyar). Nabu is prepared by dressing in the garments of "Anuship." There is a public procession for each deity from their shrine leading up to entering a bedchamber, where they spend several days in seclusion 'consummating' until (as the other rite) Nabu emerges to walk in the gardens.

Gaps in our understanding between surviving records of Old-Babylonian and Neo-Assyrian periods might be filled by some intriguing documentation of this tradition in Egypt, of all places. In this prose describing a 'bedchamber-rite', the name Nanaya is written "Nana" (or *Nanai*). However, all of the poetry-dialogue is presumably spoken by her (unidentified) "male beloved"—and it reads:

Nana, you are my wife.
The bed of rushes they have laid down,
perfumed fragrances for your nostrils.
Our goddess, may you be carried,
escorted to your dear one,
let them bear you to the dear one.
In your bridal chamber a priest sings.
Nanai, bring near to me your lips.

[*Before entering the bedchamber,
the lovers stay together for a lengthy while.*]

We dwelt here in the morning;
we shall dwell here in the evening.
The chosen lad too has come.
A sound keeps you awake in the evening;
into our shrine, my […], who is coming?
A sound of harps keeps you awake
in the evening;
in the grave of my ancestor, a dirge.
A sound of lyres from the grave
keeps you awake in the evening.

[*At the appointed hour, they enter the chamber.*]

My beloved, enter the door into our house.
With my mouth, consort of our lord,
let me kiss you.
And I go and enter.
In my nostrils it is sweet;
Come, enter the perfumed hideaway.
Horus-Bethel will lay you on the bedspread;
El, on embroidered covers.
In his heavens, Mar from Rash blesses;
Mar, a blessing before Bethel everlasting:
'My sister, Marah, blessed are you, our lady.'
'Blessed are you, Had, with a blessing fit for El.'
'Blessed are you, Baal of Heaven.'
'Rebuild humanity; A cursed land rebuild;
A city of ruins rebuild.'
'Keep alive the pauper; bless the poor man.'

DEFILEMENT OF THE RITES

Periods of Babylonian abundance and prosperity
were offset by reigns of *anti-Mardukite* rulers and
usurpers. During times of political turbulence, the
"rites were not observed" and civilization suffered.
When they were not sabotaging Mardukite religious tradition by oppressing temples or rein-
stalling archaic (*Sumerian*) cults, some of these
tyrannical kings went as far as to blatantly defile

the sacred '*bedchamber rites*' for their own sexual gratification (and to confuse the spiritual nature of such traditions, and the proper identity of deities, in social consciousness). Nabû-šumu-iškun ruled Babylonia 760 to 748 BCE. He "removed the gods from their proper places" in order to directly interfere with the Nabu – Nanaya – Tašmetu '*love triangle*' (during an era when *all three* were recognizably worshiped as a '*triad*'). He detained Nabu in Babylon, meanwhile making Nanaya "the lover of Nabû" enter the "workshop" (*bit mummu*). He "covered the '*garment*' of Nabu with the '*garment*' of Bel (Marduk)" in the eleventh month (*Shebat*). Then he, *himself*, dressed up as Bel and —*aššuta ša Bel ana Tašmetum ušatriš*—"as Bel, proposed marriage to Tašmetu!"

Nabû-šumu-iškun made it appear as though Nanaya had replaced Tašmetu in the "workshop" (presumably in Borsippa); whereas Nabû, impersonated *by* the king and falsely dressed *as* Marduk, was betrothed to Tašmetu in Babylon. Thus, Nanaya was left alone in Borsippa; whereas Tašmetu was married off to quasi-Marduk (the king in disguise) and forced to play out the role of consort to the patron god of Babylon; all the while their actual 'true love' was imprisoned and helpless to intervene. In this wise, Nabû-šumu-iškun blurred the divine roles and identities, cheated the goddesses of their proper worship, and publicly desecrated the sacred rituals of divine love.

⚜ 7 ⚜
CUNEIFORM TABLETS,
EPICS & POEMS

The following is a small collection of translated cuneiform tablet-records selected as a reference for this volume. Most of these do not already appear in the 'Mardukite Tablet Catalogue' (Esoteric Library). A few already appear in 'The Complete Anunnaki Bible', but were not included in any previous 'New Standard Zuist Editions'. [Refer to 'The Complete Anunnaki Bible' for a more comprehensive study of cuneiform literature.]

ENKI'S JOURNEY TO NIBRU

In those remote days, when the fates were determined; in a year when Anu brought about abundance, and people broke through the earth like green plants—then the lord of the *abzu*, King Enki; Enki, the lord who determines the fates, built up his temple entirely from silver and lapis lazuli. Its silver and lapis lazuli were like shining daylight. Into the shrine of the *abzu* he brought joy.

Anu artfully made bright crenellations rising out from the *abzu*, for Lord Nudimmud (another title for Enki) it was erected. He built the temple from precious metal, decorated it with lapis lazuli, and covered it abundantly with gold. In *E.ri-dug* (*Eri-*

du), he built the house on the bank. Its brickwork makes utterances and gives advice. Its eaves roar like a bull; the Temple of Enki bellows. During the night the temple praises its lord and offers its best for him. Before Lord Enki, Isimud, the minister praises the temple; he goes to the temple and speaks to it. He goes to the brick building and addresses it: "Temple, built from precious metal and lapis lazuli; whose foundation pegs are driven into the *abzu*; which has been cared for by the prince in the *abzu*! Like the Tigris and the Euphrates, it is mighty and awe-inspiring. Joy has been brought into Enki's *abzu*."

"Your lock has no rival. Your bolt is a fearsome lion. Your roof beams are the bull of heaven, an artfully made bright headgear. Your reed-mats are like lapis lazuli, decorating the roof-beams. Your vault is a wild bull raising its horns. Your door is a lion who seizes a man. Your stairway is a lion coming down on a man."

"*Abzu*, pure place which fulfills its purpose! *E.engura*! Your lord has directed his steps towards you. Enki, lord of the *abzu*, has embellished your foundation pegs with carnelian. He has adorned you with [...] and lapis lazuli. The Temple of Enki is provisioned with holy wax; it is a bull obedient to its master, roaring by itself and giving advice at the same time. *E.engura*, which Enki has surrounded with a holy reed fence, in your midst a lofty throne is erected; your door-jamb is the holy locking bar of heaven."

"Abzu, pure place, place where the fates are determined—the lord of wisdom, Lord Enki; the lord who determines the fates, Nudimmud, the lord of *E.ri-dug* lets nobody look into its midst. Your abga priests let their hair down their backs."

"Enki's beloved *E.ri-dug*; *E.engura* whose inside is full of abundance! *Abzu*, life of the Land, beloved of Enki! Temple built on the edge, befitting the artful divine powers! *E.ri-dug* your shadow extends over the midst of the sea! Rising sea without a rival; mighty awe-inspiring river which terrifies the Land! *E-engura*, high citadel standing firm on the earth! Temple at the edge of the *engur*, a lion in the midst of the *abzu*; lofty Temple of Enki, which bestows wisdom on the Land; your cry, like that of a mighty rising river, reaches King Enki."

"He made {the lyre, the *aljar*-instrument, the *balaj*-drum (of your *sur*-priests) with the drumsticks}, the *harhar*, the *sabitum*, and the [...] *miritum*-instruments offer their best for his holy temple. The [...] resounded by themselves with a sweet sound. The holy *aljar*-instrument of Enki played for him on his own and seven {singers sang and} *tigi*-drums resounded."

"What Enki says is irrefutable; [...] is well established." This is what Isimud spoke to the brick

building; he praised the E-engura {with sweet
songs} duly. As it has been built, as it has been
built; as Enki has raised *E.ri-dug* up, it is an artfully built mountain which floats on the water. His
shrine spreads out into the reed beds; birds brood
(at night) in its green orchards laden with fruit.
The *suhur*-carp play among the honey-herbs, and
the *ectub*-carp dart among the small *gizi*-reeds.
When Enki rises, the fish rise before him like
waves. He has the *abzu* stand as a marvel, as he
brings joy into the *engur*.

Like the sea, he is awe-inspiring; like a mighty
river, he instils fear. The Euphrates rises before
him as it does before the fierce south wind. His
punting pole is Nirah {*or* Imdudu *in some versions*}; his oars are the small reeds. When Enki
embarks, the year will be full of abundance. The
ship departs of its own accord, with tow rope
{held} by itself. As he leaves the Temple of *E.ri-
dug*, the river {gurgles} to its lord: its sound is a
calf's mooing; the mooing of a good cow.

Enki had offering laid lavishly. Where there were
no *ala*-drums, he installed some in their places;
where there were no bronze *ub*-drums, he dispatched some to their places. He directed his steps
on his own to Nibru and entered the temple terrace, the shrine of Nibru. Enki (reached for) the
beer, he (reached for) the liquor. He had liquor
poured into big bronze containers, and had *emmer-*

wheat beer (pressed out). In *kukuru*-containers which make the beer good, he mixed beer-mash. By adding date-syrup to taste, he made it strong. He [...] its bran-mash.

In the shrine of Nibru, Enki provided a meal for Enlil, his father. He seated Anu at the head of the table and seated Enlil next to Anu. He seated Nin-tur (Nintud) in the place of honour and seated the *Anuna* (*Anunnaki*) gods at the (adjacent places). All of them were drinking and enjoying beer and liquor. They filled the bronze *aga*-vessels to the brim and started a competition, drinking from the bronze vessels of *Urac*. They made the *tilim-da*-vessels shine like holy barges. After beer and liquor had been libated and enjoyed, and after [...] from the house, Enlil was made happy in Nibru.

Enlil addressed the Anuna gods: "Great gods who are standing here! Anuna, who have lined up in the *Ubcu-unkena* (Palace of the Assembly)! My son, King Enki has built up the temple! He has made *E.ri-dug* {rise up} {come out} from the ground like a mountain! He has built it in a pleasant place, in *E.ri-dug*, the pure place, where no one is to enter—a temple built with silver and decorated with lapis lazuli, a house which tunes the seven *tigi*-drums properly, and provides incantations; where holy songs make all of the house a lovely place—the shrine of the *abzu*, the good destiny of Enki, befitting the elaborate divine powers; the temple of *E.ri-dug*, built with silver: for all this, Father Enki be praised!"

ENKI AND NINMAH

In those days, in the days when heaven and earth were created; In those nights, in the nights when heaven and earth were created; In those years, in the years when the fates were determined; when the *Anuna* (*Anunnaki*) gods were born; When the goddesses were taken in marriage; When the goddesses were distributed in heaven and earth; When the goddesses became pregnant and gave birth; When the gods were {obliged} their food [...] dining halls. The senior gods oversaw the work, while the minor gods bore the toil. The gods were digging the canals and piling up the silt in Harali. The gods, crushing the clay, began complaining about this life.

At that time, the one of great wisdom, the creator of all the senior gods, Enki lay on his bed, not waking up from his sleep, in the deep *engur*; in the subterranean water, the place inside of which no other god knows. The gods said, weeping: "He is the cause of the lamenting!" Namma, the primeval mother who gave birth to the senior gods, took the tears of the gods to the one who lay sleeping, to the one who did not wake up from his bed, to her son: "Are you really lying there asleep, and not awake? The gods, your creatures, are smashing their [...] My son, wake up from your bed! Please apply the skill deriving from your wisdom and create a {substitute} for the gods, so that they can be freed from their toil!"

At the word of his mother Namma, Enki rose up from his bed. In *Hal-an-kug*, his room for pondering, he slapped his thigh in annoyance. The wise and intelligent one, the prudent, [...] of skills, fashioner of the design of everything brought to life {by birth-goddesses}. Enki reached out his arm over them and turned his attention to them. And after Enki, the fashioner of designs by himself, had considering the matter, he said to his mother Namma: "My mother, the creature you planned really will come into existence. Impose on him the work of carrying baskets. You should knead clay from the top of the *abzu*; the {birth-goddesses} will nip off the clay, and you shall bring the form into existence. Let Ninmah act as your assistant; and let Ninimma, Cu-zi-ana, Ninmada, Ninbarag, Ninmug, [...] and Ninguna stand by as you give birth. My mother, after you have decreed his fate, let Ninmah impose on him the work of carrying baskets."

[...] she placed it on grass and purified the birth. Enki [...] brought joy to their heart. He set a feast for his mother Namma and for Ninmah. All the courtly {royal} birth-goddesses ate delicate [...] and bread. Anu, Enlil, and Lord Nudimmud (Enki) celebrated the offering feast. All the senior gods praised him: "O lord of wide understanding, who is as wise as you? Enki, the great lord, who can equal your actions? Like a corporeal father, you are the one who has the *ME* of deciding destinies, in fact you are the *ME*."

Enki and Ninmah drank beer, their hearts became elated, and then Ninmah said to Enki: "Hunan bodies could be made either good or bad; and whether I make its fate good or bad depends on my will." Enki answered Ninmah: "I will counter-balance whatever fate—good or bad—you happen to decide."

Ninmah took clay from the top of the *abzu* in her hand and she fashioned it: First, a man who could not bend his outstretched weak hands. Enki looked at the man and decreed his fate: he appointed him as a servant of the king.

Second, she fashioned one who {"turned back the light"(?)}, a man with permanently opened eyes. Enki looked at the man and decreed his fate: allotting to it the musical arts, making him as the chief [...] in the king's presence.

Third, she fashioned one with both feet broken, with paralyzed feet {*or* "born as an idiot" *in some versions*}. Enki looked at him, and decided the work of [...] and the silversmith [...]

Fourth, she fashioned one who could not hold back his urine. Enki looked at this one and bathed him in enchanted water; he drove out the *namtar*-demon from his body. Fifth, she fashioned a woman who could not give birth. Enki looked at the woman and decreed her fate: he made her serve in the queen's household as a weaver. Sixth, she fashioned one with neither penis nor vagina. Enki looked at this one and named it {eunuch}, and decreed as its fate to stand before the king.

Ninmah {*or* Enki *in some versions*} threw (all) the pinched-off clay to the ground and was greatly [...] The great lord Enki said to Ninmah: "I have decreed the fates of your creatures and given them their daily bread. Now come, I will fashion somebody for you, and you must decree the fate of this newborn one!"

Enki devised a shape with head, [...] and mouth in its middle, and said to Ninmah: "Pour ejaculated semen into a woman's womb, and the woman will give birth from the semen." Ninmah stood by for the newborn [...] and the woman brought forth in the midst [...] As a result, this was *Umul*: its head was afflicted, its place of [...] was afflicted, its eyes were afflicted, its neck was afflicted. It could hardly breathe, its ribs were shaky, its lungs were afflicted, its heart was afflicted, its bowels were afflicted. With its hand and its lolling head, it could not not put bread into its mouth; its spine and head were dislocated. The weak hips and the shaky feet could not {carry} it on the field [...] Enki fashioned it in this way.

Enki said to Ninmah: "For your creatures I have decreed a fate, I have given them their daily bread. Now, you should decree a fate for my creature, give him his daily bread too." Ninmah looked at *Umul* and turned to him. She went nearer to *Umul*, asked him questions, but he could not speak. She offered him bread to eat, but he could not reach out for it. He could not lie on [...], he could not [...] Standing up; he could not sit down, could not lie down, he could not [...] a house, and he could not eat bread. Ninmah answered Enki: "The man you have fashioned is neither alive nor dead. He cannot support himself."

Enki answered Ninmah: "I decreed a fate for the first man with the weak hands, I gave him bread. I decreed a fate for the man who turned away from the light (who could not close his eyes), I gave him bread. I decreed a fate for the man with broken, paralyzed feet, I gave him bread. I decreed a fate for the man who could not hold back his urine, I gave him bread. I decreed a fate for the woman who could not give birth, I gave her bread. I decreed the fate for the one with neither penis nor vagina on its body, I gave it bread. My sister, [...]"

{Tablet damage; indecipherable lines omitted.}

Ninmah answered Enki: "You entered [...] [...] Look, you do not dwell in heaven, you do not dwell on earth, you do not come out to look at the Land. Where you do not dwell, but where my house is built, your words cannot be heard. Where you do not live, but where my city is built, I my-self am {silenced}. My city is ruined, my house is destroyed, my child has been taken captive. I am a fugitive who has had to leave the *E.kur*, even I my-self could not escape from your hand."

Enki replied to Ninmah: "Who could change the words that left your mouth? Remove *Umul* from your lap [...] Ninmah, may your work be [...], you [...] for me what is imperfect; who can {oppose} this? The man whom I shaped [...] after you [...], let him pray! Today let my penis be praised, may your wisdom be {confirmed}! May the *enkum* and *ninkum* [...] proclaim your glory [...] My sister, the heroic strength [...] The song [...] the writing [...] The gods who heard [...] let *Umul* build {*or* serve *?*} my house [...]" And Ninmah could not rival the great lord Enki; Father Enki, your praise is sweet!

NINGISHZIDA'S JOURNEY TO THE UNDERWORLD

"Arise and get on board; Arise, we are about to sail; Arise and get on board!" -- Woe, weep for the bright daylight, as the barge is steered away! -- "I am a young man! Let me not be covered against my wishes by a cabin, as if with a blanket; As if with a blanket!"

Stretching out a hand to the barge, to the young man being steered away on the barge; Stretching out a hand to Lord Ningishzida being taken away on the barge; Stretching out a hand to *Ictaran* of the bright visage, being taken away on the barge; Stretching out a hand to *Alla*, master of the {battle-net}, being taken away on the barge; Stretching out a hand to *Lugal-cud-e* being taken away on the barge.

Stretching out a hand to Ningishzida being taken away on the barge--his younger sister was crying in lament to him in the cabin at the boat's bow. His older sister removed the cover from the cabin at the boat's stern: "Let me sail away with you; Let me sail away with you, my brother. My brother, let me sail on your barge with you; My brother, let me sail away with you. Let me sail on your splendid barge with you, my brother." She was crying a lament to him at the boat's bow: "My brother, let me sail away with you. The *gudug* priest sits in the cabin at your boat's stern. Let me sail away with you, my brother; Let me sail away with you."

"My young man, *Damu*, let me sail away with you, my brother; let me sail away with you. *Ictar-*

an of the bright visage, let me sail away with you, my brother; let me sail away with you. *Alla*, master of the {battle-net}, let me sail away with you, my brother; let me sail away with you. *Lugal-cud-e*, let me sail away with you, my brother; let me sail away with you. *Lugal-ki-bura*, let me sail away with you, my brother; let me sail away with you. Ningishzida, let me sail away with you, my brother; let me sail away with you. My brother, let me sail on your barge with you; my brother, let me sail away with you. Let me sail on your splendid barge with you, my brother; let me sail away with you."

The evil-demon who was in their midst called out to Ningishzida: "*Lugal-ki-bura*, look at your sister!" Having looked at his sister, *Lugal-ki-bura* said to her: "He sails with me, he sails with me; Why should you (want to) sail to the underworld? Lady, the demon sails with me; Why should you sail to the underworld? The thresher sails with me; Why should you sail to the underworld? The man who has bound my hands sails with me; Why should you sail? The man who has tied my arms sails with me; Why should you sail?"

"The river of the underworld produces no water, no water is drunk from it; Why should you sail? The fields of the underworld produce no grain, no flour is eaten from it; Why should you sail? The sheep of the nether world produce no wool, no cloth is woven from it; Why should you sail? Even for me, even if my mother were to dig a canal, I shall not be able to drink the water meant for me. The waters of springtime will not be poured for me as they are for the tamarisks; I shall not sit in the shade intended for me. The dates I should bear like a date palm will not reveal their beauty for me. I am a field threshed by my demon; you would scream at it. He has put manacles on my hands; you would scream at it. He has put a neck-stock (around) my neck; you would scream at it."

Ama-cilama said to her brother, Ningishzida: "The ill-intentioned {*or* evil} demon may accept something; there should be a limit to it for you. My brother, your demon may accept something; there should be a limit to it for you. For him let me [...] from my hand the [...]; there should be a limit to it for you. For him let me [...] from my hand the [...]; there should be a limit to it for you. For him let me [...] from my hips the dainty lapis lazuli beads; there should be a limit to it for you. For him let me [...] from my hips the [...] my lapis lazuli beads; there should be a limit to it for you."

"You are a beloved [...]; there should be a limit to it for you. How they treat you; Oh, how they treat you! There should be a limit to it for you. My brother, how they treat you, how haughtily they treat you! There should be a limit to it for you. (You say) 'I am hungry, but the bread has slipped away from me'; there should be a limit to it for you. (You say) 'I am thirsty, but the water has slipped away from me'; there should be a limit to it for you."

The evil-demon who was in their midst, the clever demon, that great demon who was in their midst, called out to the man at the boat's bow and to the man at the boat's stern: "Don't let the mooring stake be pulled out, so that she may come on board to her brother; that this lady may come on board the barge."

When *Ama-cilama* had gone on board the barge, a cry approached the heavens, a cry approached the earth, that great demon set up an enveloping cry before him on the river: "*Urim*, at my cry to the heavens lock your houses, lock your houses; city, lock your houses! *Urim*, against your lord who has left the [...] city, lock your houses!" [...] a holy sceptre. [...] a holy robe of office. [...] a holy crown. [...] a lapis-lazuli sceptre. He [...] to the empty river, the rejoicing river: "You (*Ama-cilima*) shall not draw near to this house, [...] to the place (*or* palace) of *Ereshkigal* (*Eres-ki-gala*). My mother [...] out of her love. As for you (demon), you may be a great demon [...], [...] your hand against the office of the underworld's throne-bearer."

"My king will no longer shed tears in his eyes. The drum will [...] his joy in tears. Come! May the fowler utter a lament for you in his well-stocked house, lord, may he utter a lament for you. How he has been humiliated! May the young fisherman utter a lament for you in his well-stocked house, lord, may he utter a lament for you. How he has been humiliated! May the mother of the dead *gudug* priest utter a lament for you in her empty [...], utter a lament for you, lord, may she utter a lament for you. How he has been humiliated! May the mother high priestess utter a lament for you who have left the [...], lord, may she utter a lament for you. How he has been humiliated!"

"My king, bathe with water, your head that has rolled in the dust. [...] in sandals, your feet defiled from the defiled place." The king bathed with water his head that had rolled in the dust. [...] in sandals, his feet defiled from the defiled place. "Not drawing near to this house, [...] your throne [...] to you 'Sit down'. May your bed [...] to you 'Lie down'." He ate food in his mouth; he drank fine wine. Great holy one, Ereshkigal, praising you is sweet.

EPIC OF NERGAL AND ERESHKIGAL
[Akhenaton's (Amarna) Fragments]
(*From 'The Complete Anunnaki Bible' Tablet-U Series*)

When the gods organized a banquet, they sent a messenger to their sister Ereshkigal. "We cannot come down to you, and you cannot come up to us.

So, send someone to fetch a share of the food for you!"

Ereshkigal sent Namtar, her vizier: "Go up, Namtar, to high heaven!" He went into where the gods were sitting, and they bowed and greeted Namtar, the messenger of their eldest sister. They bowed respectfully when they saw him and the great gods. [. . .] food for the goddess his mistress. [. . .] wept and was overcome. [. . .] the journey.

[6+ *lines missing*]

Ea-Enki [. . .] and went to Namtar and sent him back. "Go and tell my word to our sister. She will say, 'Where is the one who did not rise to his feet in the presence of my messenger? Bring him to me for his death, that I may kill him!'"

Namtar came back and spoke to the gods, the gods summoned him and discussed the death with him. "Look for the god who did not rise to his feet in your presence, and take him before your mistress!"

Namtar counted them. The last god was crouching down. "That god who did not rise to his feet in your presence; he is not here!" Then Namtar went and gave his report, "My mistress, I went and counted them. The last god was crouching down. The god who did not rise to his feet in my presence was not there."

[*several lines missing*]

"Identify the one," [. . .] to the hand of Ea-Enki. "Take him to Ereshkigal!" He was weeping. Before his father ENKI, he pleaded: "He will see me! He will not let me stay alive!"

"Don't be afraid for I shall give to you seven [and seven] demons. To go with you I send: Lightning-Bolt, The Bailiff, The Croucher, Explosion, Terrible Wind, Fits of Sickness, The Stagger, The Stroke, The Lord of the Roof, The Fever, The Scab and [. . .] Ereshkigal will call out, 'Gatekeeper, [. . .] open your door.'"

[several lines missing]

Nergal approaches the gates: "Loosen the lock, that I may enter into the presence of your mistress, Ereshkigal. I have been sent from above!"

The Gatekeeper said to Namtar: "A god is standing at the entrance of the door. Come, inspect him and let him enter." Namtar came out, saw him and called: "Wait here!" He went to his mistress and said: "My lady, here is the god who in previous months had vanished, and who did not rise to his feet in my presence above!"

Ereshkigal replied: "Bring him in. As soon as he comes, I shall kill him!" Namtar came out and addressed Nergal: "Come in, my lord, to your sister's house and [. . .]" Nergal said, "You should be glad to see me. . .

[*several lines missing*]

...At the seventh, the Terrible Wind. At the eighth, Fits of Sickness. At the ninth, The Staggers. At the tenth, The Stroke. At the eleventh, The Lord of the Roof. At the twelfth, The Fever. At the thirteenth, The Scab. At the fourteenth Gate, he managed to seal her in. In the forecourt he cut off Namtar. He gave his troops the orders: "Let the doors be opened! Now I shall race past you!"

Inside the house, he seized Ereshkigal by her hair, pulled her from the throne to the ground, intending to cut off her head. "Don't kill me, my brother! Let me tell you something."

Nergal listened to her and relaxed his grip, he wept and was overcome when she said: "You can be my husband, and I can be your wife. I will let you seize Kingship over the wide Earth! I will put the Tablet of Destiny in your hand! You can be the master; I can be the mistress."

Nergal listened to this speech of hers, and seized her and kissed her. He wiped away her tears. "These things have you asked of me? After so many months, it shall certainly be so!"

COURTSHIP OF ISHTAR & DUMUZI
(*From 'The Complete Anunnaki Bible' Tablet-U Series*)

The brother spoke to his younger sister. The Sun

God, Shammash {Utu}, spoke to Inanna {Ishtar}, saying: "Lady, the flax in its fullness is lovely. Inanna {Ishtar}, the grain is glistening in the furrow. I will work the ground for you. I will bring the grain to you. But a piece of linen-cloth, big or small, is always needed. Inanna {Ishtar}, I will bring it to you."

Inanna said: "Brother, after you've brought me the flax, who will comb it for me?" Shammash {Utu} replied: "Sister, I will bring it to you combed."

Inanna said: "Shammash {Utu}, after you've brought it to me combed, who will spin it for me?" Shammash {Utu} responded: "Inanna {Ishtar}, I will bring it to you spun."

Inanna said: "Brother, after you've brought the flax to be spun, who will braid it for me?" And Shammash {Utu} responded: "Sister, I will bring it to you braided."

Inanna {Ishtar} said: "Shammash {Utu}, after you've brought it to me braided, who will weave it for me?" And Shammash {Utu} replied: "Sister, I will bring it to you woven."

Inanna {Ishtar} said: "Shammash {Utu}, after you've brought it to me woven; who will bleach it for me?" Shammash {Utu} responds: "Inanna {Ishtar}, I will bring it to you bleached."

Angered now, Inanna {Ishtar} demanded: "Brother, after you've brought my bridal sheet to me, who will go to bed with me!? Who, Shammash {Utu} —who will sleep with me!?" Shammash {Utu} calmly replied: "Sister, your bridegroom will go to bed with you. He who was born from a fertile womb; He who was conceived on the sacred marriage throne, Dumuzi, the shepherd! He will go to bed with you."

Inanna {Ishtar} spoke: "No, brother! I want the farmer! He is the man of my heart! He gathers the grain into great heaps. He brings the grain regularly into my storehouses." Shammash {Utu} said: "Sister, you should marry the shepherd. Why are you unwilling? His *cream* is good; his *milk* is good. Whatever he touches shines brightly. Inanna {Ishtar}, marry Dumuzi. You who adorn yourself with the agate necklace of fertility alone, why are you unwilling? Dumuzi will share his rich *cream* with you. You who are meant to be the king's protector; why are you unwilling?"

Still angry, Inanna {Ishtar} then spoke: "The shepherd?! I will not marry the shepherd! His clothes are course; his wool is rough. I will marry the farmer. The farmer grows flax for my clothes, the farmer grows barley for my table."

Then Dumuzi arrived and said: "Why do you speak about the farmer? Why do you speak about him? If he gives you black flour, I will give you black wool. If he gives you white flour, I will give you white wool. If he gives you beer, I will give you sweet milk. If he gives you bread, I will give you honey cheese. I will give the farmer my leftover cream. I will give the farmer my leftover milk. Why do you speak about the farmer? What does he have more than I do?"

Laughing, Inanna {Ishtar} replied: "Shepherd-boy, without my mother, Ningal, you'd be driven away; without my grandmother, Ningikugga, you'd be driven to the *Abyss*; without my father, Nanna-Sin, you'd have no roof; without my brother Shammash {Utu} [...]"

Dumuzi interrupted: "Inanna {Ishtar}, do not start a quarrel with me. My father, Enki, is as good as your father, Nanna. My mother, Sirtur, is as good as your mother, Ningal. My sister, Geshtinanna, is as good as yours, Ereshkigal [...] So, Queen of the palace, let us talk it over, shall we?"

The words they had spoken between them were words of passion and desire. From the start of the heated quarrel came the lovers' desire for each other.

Dumuzi, The Shepherd, went to the royal house with cream. He went to the royal house with milk. Before the door, he called out: "Open the house, My Lady, open the house!"

Inanna {Ishtar} ran to the arms of Ningal, her mother. Ningal counseled her daughter, saying: "My child, this young man will be your father. My daughter, this young man will be your mother. He will treat you like a father. He will care for you like a mother." Still Dumuzi called: "Open the house, My Lady, open the house!"

Inanna {Ishtar}, at her mother's command, bathed and anointed herself with scented oil. She covered her body with the royal white robe. She readied her dowry. She arranged her precious lapis lazuli beads around her neck. She took her seal in her hand. Dumuzi waited expectantly. Inanna {Ishtar} opened the door for him. Inside the house she shined before him. Like the light of the moon. Dumuzi looked at her joyously. He pressed his neck close against hers. He kissed her.

Inanna {Ishtar} then said: "What I tell you, let the singer weave into song. What I tell you, let it flow from ear to mouth, let it pass from old to young: My vulva, the horn, is The Boat of Heaven; is full of eagerness like the new moon. Who will plow my vulva? Who will plow my high field? Who will plow my wet ground? I am a young beautiful woman; Who will plow my vulva!? Who will station the ox there!? Who will plow my vulva!?"

Dumuzi smiled and said: "Great Lady, the king will plow your vulva! I, Dumuzi the King, will plow your vulva." Inanna {Ishtar} screamed: "Then plow my vulva, man of my heart! Plow my vulva! Do it now!"

* * *

When after the king's lap stood the rising cedar. Plants grew high by their side. Grains grew high by their side. Gardens flourished luxuriantly.

Inanna {Ishtar} sang in delight: "He has sprouted; He is fertile growth planted by the water. He is the one my womb loves best. My well-stocked garden in the plains, my barley growing high in its furrow, my apple tree which bears fruit up to its crown; he is fertile growth planted by the water. My honey-man, my honey-man sweetens me always. My lord, the honey-man of the gods; He is the one my womb loves best. His hand is honey, his foot is honey; He sweetens me always. My eager man who caresses my navel; My man who caresses my soft thighs, he is the one my womb loves best. O, how I love him! He is my fertile growth planted by the water."

And Dumuzi sang: "O Great Lady, your breast is your field. Inanna {Ishtar}, your breast is your field. Your broad field pours out the plants. Your broad field pours out grain. Water flows from on high for your servant. Bread flows from on high for your servant. Pour it out for me, Inanna {Ishtar}. I will drink all you offer."

Inanna {Ishtar} said passionately: "Make your milk sweet and thick for me, my bridegroom. My shepherd, I will drink your fresh milk. My wild bull, Dumuzi, make your milk sweet and thick. I will drink your fresh milk. Let the milk of the goat flow in my sheepfold. Fill my holy churn with honey cheese. Lord Dumuzi, I will drink your fresh milk. My husband, I will guard my sheepfold for you. I will watch over your house of life, the storehouse; The shining quivering place which delights; The house which decides the fates of the land; The house which gives the breath of life to the people. I, the queen of the palace, will watch over your house."

Dumuzi spoke: "My sister, I would go with you to my garden. Inanna {Ishtar}, I would go with you to my garden. I would go with you to my orchard. I would go with you to my apple tree. There I would plant the sweet, honey-covered seed."

Inanna {Ishtar} sang: "He brought me into his garden. My brother, Dumuzi, brought me into his garden. I strolled with him among the standing trees, I stood with him among the fallen trees, by the apple tree I knelt as is proper. Before my brother coming in song; who rose to me out of poplar leaves; who came to me in the midday heat, before my lord, Dumuzi, I poured out plants from my womb. I placed plants before him; I poured out plants before him. I placed grain before him; I poured out grain before him; I poured out grain before my womb."

She sang louder: "Last night as I, the Queen, was shining bright; Last night as I, the Queen of Heaven, was shining bright; As I was shining bright and dancing; Singing praises at the coming of the night; He met me! He met me! My lord Dumuzi met me! He pushed his hand to my hand. He pressed his neck close against mine. My high priest is ready for the holy loins. My lord Dumuzi is ready for the holy loins. The plants and herbs in his field are ripe. Dumuzi! Your fullness is my delight!"

She called for it, she called for it, she called for the bed! She called for the bed that rejoices the heart. She called for the bed that sweetens the loins. She called for the bed of kingship. She called for the bed of queenship. Inanna {Ishtar} called for the bed: "Let the bed that rejoices the heart be prepared! Let the bed that sweetens the loins be prepared! Let the bed of kingship be prepared! Let the bed of queenship be prepared! Let the royal bed be prepared!" She spread the bridal sheet across the bed. She called to the king: "The bed is ready!" She called to her bridegroom: "The bed is waiting!"He put his hand in her hand. He put his heart to her heart. Sweet is the sleep of the hand-to-hand. Sweeter still is the sleep of heart-to-heart.

Inanna {Ishtar} said: "I bathed for the wild bull, I bathed for the shepherd Dumuzi, I perfumed my sides with ointment, I coated my mouth with sweet-smelling amber, I painted my eyes with coal. He shaped my loins with his fair hands. The Shepherd, Dumuzi filled my lap with cream and milk; He stroked my pubic hair; He watered my womb. He laid his hands on my holy vulva; He smoothed my black boat with cream; He quickened my narrow boat with milk; He caressed me on the bed. Now I will caress my high priest on the bed, I will caress the faithful shepherd Dumuzi, I will caress his loins, the shepherdship of the land, I will decree a sweet fate for him."

'SUMMER' & 'WINTER'
(Sumerian 'Emesh & Enten' Cycle)

Anu lifted his head in pride and brought forth a good day. He laid plans for [...] and spread (wide) [...] the population. Enlil set his foot upon the earth like a great bull. Enlil, the king of all lands, set his mind to increasing the good day of abundance: to making the [...] night resplendent in celebration; to making flax grow; to making barley proliferate; to guaranteeing the spring floods at the quay; to making [...] lengthen their days in abundance; to making Summer close the sluices of heaven; and to making Winter guarantee plentiful water at the quay.

He copulated with the great hills; he gave the mountain its share. He filled its womb with Summer and Winter, the plenitude and life of the land. As Enlil copulated with the earth, there was a war {like a bull's}. The hill spent the day at that place and at night she opened her loins. She bore Summer and Winter as smoothly as fine oil. He fed them pure plants on the terraces of the hills like great bulls. He nourished them in the pasture of the hills.

Enlil set about determining the destinies of Summer and Winter. For Summer: founding towns and villages; bring in harvests of plenitude for the Great Mountain, Enlil; sending laborers out to the large arable tracts; and working the fields with oxen. For Winter: plenitude; the spring floods; the abundance and life of the land; placing grain in the fields and fruitful acres; and gathering in everything. Enlil determined these as the destinies of Summer and Winter.

Winter guided the spring floods, the abundance and life of the land, down from the edge of the hills. He set his foot upon the Tigris and Euphrates (like a big bull) and released them into the fields and fruitful acres of Enlil. He shaped lagoons in the water of the sea. He surrounded all the reed-beds with mature reeds, reed shoots and [...] reeds.

Summer, the heroic sun of Enlil, drained the large arable tracts. He [...] cool water on the fields and fruitful acres like [...] [...] Holy winter [...] The ox [...] its head in a yoke. Ninurta, Enlil's son, [...] the fruitful acres. He [...] grain in the large arable tracts. He fills the fields and fruitful acres of Enlil.

Winter made the ewe give birth to the lamb; he gave the kid to the goat. He made cows teem together with their calves; he provided butter and milk. On the high plain he made the deer and stag glad of heart. He made the birds of heaven set their nests in broad spaces. The fish of the lagoons laid eggs in the reed-bed. In all the orchards he made honey and wine drip to the ground. He made the trees, wherever planted, bear fruit. He established gardens and provided plants. He made grain abundant in the furrows. He made *Ezina* appear radiant as a beautiful maiden. The harvest, the great festival of Enlil, rose heavenward.

Summer founded houses and farmsteads, he made the cattle-pens and sheepfolds wide. He multiplied the stacks of sheaves in all the arable tracts. At their edge he made [...] flax [...] ripen. He brought a plentiful harvest into the temples; he heaped up piles of grain. He founded towns and villages; he built the houses of the land. He made the houses of the gods grow like the hills in a pure place. In *E.-namtila*, the holy seat of kingship, fit for high daises; he established abundance for the Great Mountain, Enlil.

Summer, the heroic son of Enlil, decided to bring offerings to *E.namtila*, the house of Enlil. He brought animals, cattle and sheep of the hill, fully grown wild rams, deer and stags, [...] sheep, long-fleeced barley-fed sheep, thick-tailed sheep. Pigs grown fat in the midst of the reed-beds, porcupine, tortoise, turtle, birds brooding in their nests, taken together with their eggs, harvest crops, flour and malt for mixing, butter and milk from cattle-pen and sheepfold, wheat, [...] beans, small beans and large beans gathered in piled-high baskets, onions [...] in their furrows, *zahadin*-onions and shallots, seed turnips, saffron, [...] [...]. Summer, the heroic son of Enlil, offered.

Winter, lordly son of Enlil, [...], released the water of life and [...] opened. He gathered the [...] oxen and [...] the oxen. The disputed sheep was provided, barley-fed but with a scorpion at its side. Quartz, gold and silver found in leather pouches, cedar, cypress, [...], boxwood, [...], [...] tribute of the land, figs from Mari, [...], strings of dried fruit, cool water, the tribute of the hills, [...] thick honey, *dida*-beer, [...], village [...], *bibra*-birds *esig*-birds, *buru-bacur* birds, fattened ducks, carp, [...] which Winter made grow, large pomegranates gathered from the orchards, big bunches of grapes on high, winter cucumbers, [...] empty [...], brought forth [...] in the early rain, large turnips, large [...] cut down with the knife, long leeks. Winter himself brought the tribute he had collected.

Summer and Winter set about organizing the animals and offerings for *E.namtila*, the house of Enlil. The two of them, like huge butting bulls, reared themselves triumphantly. But Winter, because his limbs had grown tired from the grain grown heavy in the furrows, and the wheat and *emmer* which he had been watering by hand, turned away as from an enemy and would not draw near.

Consequently, Winter was overcome by anger and he started a quarrel with Summer: "Summer, my brother, you should not praise yourself; whatever harvest produce you bring as gifts to the palace has not been made by your toil: you should not brag. As if you were the one who had done the hard work; as if you had done the farming; as if you had taken care of irrigation control during the spring floods; as if you had brought forth the [...] grain in the arable tracts with the dew from heaven: how much through my toil is it that you enter the palace!"

"Whatever animals, cattle and sheep of the hill, you bring to my [...] [...] Your gardener [...] the palace [...]; Honey and wine in the orchard [...]; Its destructive hoe [...]; Your gathered vegetables, the purslane, [...]; Whatever you [...] at the gate of the palace. In the field your arm [...]. The straw of your grain you bring [...]"

"After you have threshed it at your threshing floor, and have [...] the cattle's dung, your carrying nets are to hand, [...] bearing your straw. [...] the animals, the storehouses and their contents. After your houses and farmsteads [...] sheep, [...] from your cattle, after [...] their reed-beds, after [...] green briars and cut [...] thorns, [...] storehouse [...] the dung of unyoked oxen -- the slave, Summer, the duly-appointed laborer who will never rest from his toil, a hired man who has to return to the fields of the land for his own sustenance!"

On that day Winter taunted Summer, the hero whom one does not challenge, searched for rude insults. He was confident in himself, considering the harvest time, and turned aside. Like a great bull eating rich grass, he raised his head.

Next, Summer replied to Winter: "Winter, you may have to stay by the side of the oven, [...]; but you should not launch such serious insults against someone who does not lead a {sedentary life}. [...] for the work of tilling the land, with its difficulties; you do not raise a cry in the [...] cult center; you do not look after the house. The young scribe is neglectful, which is an abomination, and no rushes are plucked for the beds. The singer does not embellish the banquet, [...] at its side."

"Winter, don't launch such insults! [...] to the desert. I will make the strength of my power come forth in the house so that you recognize it. In my working term of duty, which is seven months of the year, [...] does not speak softly. [...] [...] Tirelessly and constantly I place abundance upon the fields."

"After they [...] my seed, Winter, do not [...] noise, when water is cut off from the arable tracts, when the bowls lie placed, when the fishing place has been prepared, when the fish have been piled up, I am father Enlil's great comptroller. I harrow the fields into fruitful acres. When the oxen have stopped working in the fields, when you have concentrated your efforts on the damp areas and given the sign for the field work, I do not work for you in the large arable tracts and fruitful acres early in the season. If the spring grain bends its neck in the hollow of the furrows, no one provides a fence. Whatever your farmer brings to the oxen, he will not make the oxen angry with me. Winter [...] in the uplands [...]. The man of the bedroom [...]." Then Summer taunted Winter: "Wise [...], serious insults [...], not [...]."

Thereupon Winter replied to Summer: "Summer, the donkey grazing on grass at the harvest {ground} and braying noisily; the mule [...]; the harvest ox chafing its neck in the pegs and tossing its head in the lead rope; the innkeeper going to the harvest {ground} carrying a bowl in his hands; the flour [...] playing [...]; the bragging fieldworker who does not know the extent of the field. Summer, my brother, after you have gone out boasting about my toil, when at the turn of the year grain is brought into the houses and granaries are packed full, when you bring the surplus, your *bardul*-garment and your *niglam*-garment are [...]. When some one gives a {great axe} to you, you go off to your steppe."

"Summer, my brother, the wet spots must not be [...] when tilling the field. A man from the store-house stands in front of you and instructs you. When on the high plain [...] the ash tree [...], [...] yourself [...]. [...] When tribute is brought in your freight boats [...]. When the grass has arrived in the storehouse, [...] before me. What will the penned sheep eat? Your [...] reeds are exhausted. The reed-cutter who sets about pruning with the {machete} and splitting older reeds, the builder who places laborers in houses, never resting from his efforts, the potter who digs out clay, lights a fire and stokes it with wood [...] the pot! Weaver, weave your *bardul*-garment with the strength of your *aktum*-cloth. Brewer, bake your beer bread at the harvest {ground} as your assignment! Cook, produce great banquet loaves in summer! The building supervisor [...] the [...] of the roofs. People [...] boots and shoes [...]."

"Summer, my brother, as long as you go with my term of duty, great and small shall order you about and your string is not cut. Although you have gathered all things in the land and filled the store-houses, in all my strength, I am their owner when your limbs become tired. When the clouds have brought down the abundance of heaven, and the water of the first greening has descended from the hills, and the new grain has been put in the granary to be added to the old grain; the good farmer, having seen to his fields, shouts for joy, the carrier donkeys stand ready and he sets out confidently for the city."

"My brother, when you have put the holy plow away in the barn, the storehouse, everything you have gathered, you make a roar like fire. You sit down to plentiful food and drink. You obtain the choicest goods from the land. For my king named *Nanna*, the son of Enlil, *Ibbi-Suen*, when he is arrayed in the *cutur*-garment and the *hasag*-garment; when you have taken care of the *bardul*-garment and the *nijlam*-garment; when you have made a perfect feast for the gods; when the Anuna {*or* Anunnaki} have placed garments on their holy bodies; in his *E.namtila*, the holy abode of kingship founded by Anu, at the place of content they prepare a choice banquet."

"When the cem and ala drums, [...] and the other instruments play together for him, he passes the time with your heart-gladdening *tigi* and *zamzam*-instruments. But it is I who have made the wine plentiful and made much to eat and drink. I perfect the garments with fine oil. I bring up the [...], the *cutut* and *aktum*-garments. As for safeguarding, the best in Sumer, in the oppressive heat of Summer, where they had put away in the bedrooms amongst the 'black-haired people' {*or* humans}, moths destroy the blankets and make the *aktum*-cloth perish because of you. [...] exhausts itself for you [...]. The wooden chest [...]. I am Ninkasi's help; for her I sweeten the beer, with as much cold water, the tribute of the hills, as you brought."

"After [...] pots, after [...] pots, after the plump grapes have been laid out in the cool breeze, I make my king's great palace [...] pleasant. I am the one who cools down my king. I fill the fish-hook. My comrade, grasp your leather bag, go out [...]. The farmer [...] hardship. The farmer [...] the rain. The gardener does not know how to plant purslane, your [...] basket [...]. How can you compare yourself to me while seeking a roof under which to rest?"

For a second time Winter has taunted Summer. Summer, the heroic son of Enlil, was convinced of his own strong power and consequently trusted in himself. He acted as if in a friendly manner to the insults that Winter had spoken to him.

Then Summer replied to Winter: "Winter, you should not boast about your superior strength after you have explained the grounds for your boasting. I shall speak about your abode in the city which I shall [...] You seem like a man of (high) office, but you are an inept one. Your straw bundles are for the oven-side, hearth and kiln. Like a herdsman or shepherd encumbered by sheep and lambs, helpless people run like sheep from oven-side to kiln, and from kiln to oven-side, in the face of you. In sunshine [...] you reach decisions, but now in the city people's teeth chatter because of you."

"When the day is half done, nobody walks about the streets. The servant, basking by the side of the oven, is in the house until sunset. The maid, not attending to the flow of the water-container, passes the day (resting) on garments. As for the fields not worked in winter, their furrows are not cut straight; and their grain, having not been cast into a wholesome place, is taken away by huge flocks of rooks. The vegetable cutter [...] does not [...] those vegetables at the market. Carrying old reeds, the laborer is halt and lame. Don't speak with a gaping mouth of your superior strength; I will make known its shape and {substance}."

For a second time Summer had taunted Winter. On that day of the *E.kur*'s festival and (celebrating) *Sumer*'s plenty {*or* abundance}, the two of them stretched their legs and stood combatively. Summer and Winter, like great bulls about to tear at each other's horns, bent forward like wild bulls in the main courtyard and took their positions.

Like a great bull Winter raised his head to speak: "Father Enlil, you gave me control of irrigation; you brought plentiful water. I made one meadow adjacent to another and I heaped high the granaries. The grain became thick in the furrows. *Ezina* came forth in splendor like a beautiful maiden. Summer, a bragging field-administrator who does not know the extent of the field, [...] my thighs grown tired from toil. [...] tribute has been produced for the king's palace. Winter admires the heart of your [...] in words."

Summer pondered {*or* considered} everything in his head and calmed down. Summer spoke respectfully to Enlil: "Enlil, your verdict is highly valued, your holy word is an exalted word. The verdict you pronounce is one which cannot be altered; who can change it? There was quarreling of brother and brother but now there is harmony. For as long as you are occupying the palace, the people will express awe. When it is your season, far be it from me to humiliate you; in fact I shall praise you."

Enlil answered Summer and Winter: "Winter is the controller of the life-giving waters for all the lands; the farmer of the gods produces everything. Summer, my son, how can you compare yourself to your brother, Winter?"

The importance of the exalted word (that) Enlil speaks is skillfully made; the verdict he pronounces is one which cannot be altered; who can change it? Summer bowed to Winter and offered him a prayer. In his house he prepared *emmer*-beer and wine. At its side they spend the day at a succulent banquet. Summer presents Winter with gold, silver, and lapis lazuli. They pour out brotherhood and friendship like (the) best oil. By bringing sweet words to the quarrel they have achieved harmony with each other. In the dispute between Summer and Winter: Winter, the faithful farmer of Enlil, was superior to Summer; praise be to the Great Mountain, father Enlil.

HYMN OF THE TEMPLES
(*Sumerian—Archaic Translation*)

E.unir ('House Which is a Ziggurat'), grown together with heaven and earth, foundation of heaven and earth, great banqueting hall of *E.ridug*! *Abzu*, shrine erected for its prince, *E.du-kug* ('House which is a Holy Hill/Mound') where pure food is eaten; watered by the prince's pure canal; mountain, pure place cleansed with the potash plant; *Abzu*, your *tigi*-drums belong to the divine powers. Your great [...] wall is in good repair. Light does not enter your meeting-place where the god dwells, the great [...], the beautiful place. Your tightly constructed house is sacred and has no equal. Your prince, the great prince, has fixed firmly a holy crown for you in your precinct; *E.ri-dug* with a crown placed on your head, bringing forth thriving thorn-bushes, pure thorn-bushes for the *susbu*-priests;

O shrine *Abzu*, your place, your great place!

At your place of calling upon Utu [*Shammash*]; at your oven bringing bread to eat; on your ziggur-at, a magnificent shrine stretching toward heaven; at your great oven, rivaling the great banqueting hall, your prince, the prince of heaven and earth [...] can never be changed; the [...], the creator, the [...], the wise one, the [...]; Lord Nudimmud {*another name for* EA/Enki}, has erected a house in your precinct, *E.engura* ('House of the Subterranean Waters'), and taken his seat upon your dais. [...] the house of Enki in *E.ri-dug*.

O [...], shrine where destiny is determined, [...], foundation, raised with a ziggurat, [...], settlement of Enlil, your [...], your right and your left are *Sumer* and *Akkad*. House of Enlil, your interior is cool, your exterior determines destiny. Your door-jambs and architrave are a mountain summit, your projecting pilasters a dignified mountain. Your peak is a [...] peak of your princely platform. Your base serves heaven and earth. Your prince, the great prince Enlil, the good lord, the lord of the limits of heaven, the lord who determines destiny; the Great Mountain, Enlil, has erected a house in your precinct, O shrine *Nibru*, and taken his seat upon your dais. [...] the house of Enlil in *Nibru*.

Tummal, exceedingly worthy of the princely divine powers, inspiring awe and dread! Foundation, your pure lustration extends over the *abzu*. Primeval city, reed-bed green with old reeds and new shoots, your interior is a mountain of abundance built in plenitude. At your feast held in the month of the New Year, you are wondrously adorned as the Great Lady of *Ki-Ur* rivals Enlil. Your princess, Mother Ninlil, the beloved wife of Nunamnir, has erected a house in your precinct, *E.Tummal* ('Tummal House'), and taken a place upon your dais. [...] the house of Ninlil in Nibru.

E.melem-huc ('House of Terrifying Radiance') exuding great awesomeness, *Ec-mah* ('magnificent shrine'), to which princely divine powers were sent from heaven; storehouse of Enlil founded for the primeval divine powers, worthy of nobility, lifting your head in princeship, counselor of *E.kur*, parapeted buttress, your house [...] the platform {of} heaven. The decisions at its place of reaching the great judgment, the river of the ordeal, let the just live and consign to darkness the hearts that are evil. In your great place fit for pure lustration and the rites of *icib*-priests, you dine with Lord Nunamnir. Your prince, the prince who is the counselor of Enlil and worthy of *Ec-mah*, the *udug*-demon of *E.kur* the leader Nuska, has erected a house in your precinct, O house of Enlil, and taken his seat upon your dais. [...] the house of Nusku in *Nibru*.

E.me-ur-ana ('House Which Gathers the Divine Powers of Heaven') standing in a great place; the just divine powers which the warrior [...], strength of battle, heroic mace, carrier of the quiver, mighty bustling brick building, your foundation is eternal. Founded by the primeval lord, with decisions which belong to the princely divine powers, holy soil filling the mountain, lifting your head among the princes; magnificent house, the wonder coming from you is like the sun whose glow spreads. *E-cu-me-ca* ('House Which [...] the Divine Powers'), Enlil has instilled your name with terrifying awesomeness.

Your prince, the great [...], the warrior whose strength is boundless, the great ruler for Enlil, the noble who rivals heaven and earth, the provisioning seal-keeper of Father Enlil who makes the great divine powers perfect, the [...], the leader for Father Enlil, the foremost, the lion engendered by the Great Mountain, who destroys the hostile lands for Enlil, Lord Ninurta, has erected a house in your precinct, *E.cu-me-ca*, and taken his seat upon your dais. [...] the house of Ninurta in *Nibru*.

E.ja-duda {or *E.ga-duda*} ('House, Chamber of the Mound'), [...]; crown of the high plain, holy place, pure place, house, your foundation is a great princely mooring pole. *Du-saj-dili* {or *Du-*

sag-dili} (singular mound), your lady, the singular woman who keeps the chamber and the dais full, gladdens your platform in princely style. Your princess who avoids anger and is exceedingly wise, the princely daughter who prospers together with the Great Mountain, *Cu-zi-ana*, the junior wife of Father Enlil, has erected a house in your precinct, O *Du-saj-dili*, and taken her seat upon your dais. [...] the house of *Cu-zi-ana* in *Ja-gi-mah* {or *Ga-gi-mah*}.

O mighty *Kec*, form of heaven and earth, arousing terror like a great horned viper, house of Ninhursaga, built in a terrifying place! Respected *Kec*, your interior is a deep interior while your exterior is tall. Great lion [...] on the high plain and roving about on the plain, great hill established by incantations, twilit interior in which moonlight does not shine, Nintur has made you beautiful; O house *Kec*, your brickwork and your molding of it! Your terrace! Your exterior, a lustrous *suh*-crown, and your building of it! Your princess, the silencing princess, the true and Great Lady of heaven, when she talks heaven trembles, when she opens her mouth a storm thunders, *Aruru*, the sister of Enlil, has erected a house in your precinct, O house *Kec*, and taken her seat upon your dais. [...] the house of Ninhursaga in *Kec*.

O *Urim*, bull standing in the wet reeds, *E.kic.nu.*

jal {or *E.kic-nu-gal*} ('House Sending Light to the Earth'), calf of a great cow, [...] light of holy heaven, [...], trap laid in a nest, *Urim*, container feeding all lands, you are a shrine in a pure place, earth of Anu. House of *Su-en* {or *Nan-na-Sin*}, at your front a prince, at your back a ruler, your dining hall with *adab*-songs, your great, holy banqueting hall with *cem* and *ala*-drums! The light coming from you and your true lordship is a precious destiny.

Jipar, princely shrine of the holy divine powers, shining like the [...] sun, *E.kic.nu.jal*, beaming moonlight which comes forth in the Land, broad light of midday which fills all lands, house, your platform is a great snake, a marsh of snakes. Your foundation is the *abzu*, fifty in number, and the *engur*, seven in number, a shrine which looks into the heart of the gods. Your prince, the prince who makes decisions, the crown of wide heaven, the sovereign of heaven, *Acimbabbar*, has erected a house in your precinct, O shrine *Urim*, and taken his seat upon your dais. [...] the house of *Nanan* {Nanna} of *Urim*.

E.mu-mah ('House with a Magnificent Name'), rising mountain of heaven, your holy sides and your great foundation are a precious destiny. Interior full with princely divine powers, a beaming light which shines, shrine with your back to the blue sky and your prominent front

to all people, in the Land it represents a binding
agreement and a single track. Magnificent river
with open mouth gathering together your [...]
divine powers, your base is great in awesomeness, a righteous hill grown in a broad place.
Your lofty dwelling-place of magnificence with
all the divine powers of princeship, [...], shout-
ing [...]; house of celebration, your platform
gladdens the settlements.

House, your prince *Culgi* has made it great and
most princely. The perfect and magnificent [...],
the mighty and great wind, adorned with the divine powers, determining destiny, *Culgi* of Anu,
has erected a house in your precinct, *E.husag*
('House Which is a Hill/Mound'), and taken his
seat upon your dais. [...] *E.husag* of *Culgi* in *Urim*.

O city, [...] from the *abzu* like barley, cloudy
plain, taking the divine powers from its midst;
Kuara, your foundation and just banqueting hall,
the lord who does not hold back his goods
stands ready for admiration. The Seven Sages
have enlarged it for you from the south to the
uplands. Your prince, the most precious prince
Asarluhi {another name for *Marduk*}, the most
precious one, is a warrior, born a noble prince, a
leopard who seizes prey. He is like an onrushing
storm battering the rebel land. As long as it remains disobedient, he pours spittle upon it.
Asar-alim-nuna, the son of the *abzu*, has erected a

house in your precinct, O house *Kuara*, and taken his seat upon your dais. [...] the house of *Asarluhi* in *Kuara*.

E.gud-du-car ('House with Many Perfect Oxen') of holy *nir*-stone in which its sovereign sits, raising a magnificent door decoration for the princely son, whose best fine oil is holy and well-prepared; *Ja-bura* ('chamber of bowls'), holy cattle-pen pasturing cows with *munzer*-plants, your prince is a great wild bull, an elephant rejoicing in its own strength, a wild cow growing horns and and delighting in its shining horns. The incantation priest of opposed languages who put clouds in the sky, the storm which roars in the sky, as the sunlight giving [...] to the earth, *Ningublaga*, the son of *Nanna*, has erected a house in your precinct, *Ki-abrig*, and taken his seat upon your dais. [...] the house of *Ningublaga* on *Ki-abrig*.

O shrine, great sanctuary founded at a cattle-pen, small shining city of *Su-en* (*Nanna-Sin*), *Kar-zida* ('pure quay'), your interior is a mighty place, your foundation is holy and clean. Shrine, your jipar is founded in purity. Your door is of strong copper set up at a great place. Lowing cattle-pen, you raise your horns like a bull. Your prince, the lord of heaven standing in joy, [...] at midday and [...], *Acimbabbar*, has erected a house in your precinct, O *Kar-zida*, and taken his seat upon your dais. [...] the house of *Nanna* in *Gaec*.

O 'House Which Comes Forth From Heaven',
resplendent in *Kulaba*; shrine *E.babbar* ('shining
house'), shining bull, lift your neck to *Utu*
(*Shammash*) who [...] in the sky! Your shining
horns are aggressive, holy and lustrous. Bearing
a beard of shining lapis lazuli, [...], your prince,
the mighty sunlight, the lord who [...] the true
word, who lightens the horizon, who lightens
the sky's [...] vault, *Utu*, the sovereign of *E.bab-
bar*, has erected a house in your precinct, O
house *Larsa(m)*, and taken his seat upon your
dais. [...] the house of *Utu* in *Larsa(m)*.

E.negir, great libation pipe, libation pipe to the
underworld of Ereshkigal; *Gudua* (the '*Entrance
to the Underworld*') of Sumer where mankind is
gathered; *E.gida* ('long house'), in the land your
shadow has stretched over the princes of the
land. Your prince, the seed of the great lord, the
sacred one of the great underworld, given birth
by Ereshkigal, playing loudly on the *canaru*-in-
strument, sweet as the voice of a calf, *Ninazu* of
the words of prayer, has erected a house in your
precinct; O house *E.negir*, and taken his seat
upon your dais. [...] the house of Ninazu in *E.ne-
gir*.

O primeval place, deep mountain founded in an
artful fashion, shrine, terrifying place lying in a
pasture, a dread whose lofty ways none can

fathom, *Jicbanda* (?), neck-stock, meshed net, shackles of the great underworld from which none can escape, your exterior is raised up, prominent like a snare, your interior is where the sun rises, endowed with wide-spreading plenty. Your prince is the prince who stretches out his pure hand, the holy one of heaven, with luxuriant and abundant hair hanging at his back, Lord Ningishzida. Ningishzida has erected a house in your precinct; O *Jicbanda*, and taken his seat upon your dais. [...] the house of Ningishzida in *Jicbanda*.

O house with the great divine powers of *Kulaba*, [...], its platform has made the great shrine flourish. Green fresh fruit, marvelous, filled with ripeness, descending from the centre of heaven, shrine built for the bull, *E.ana* (or *E.anna*; 'House of Heaven'), house with seven corners, with seven fires lifted at night-time, surveying seven pleasures, your princess is on the pure horizon. Your lady Inanna {or Ishtar} who [...], who adorns the woman and covers the man's head with a cloth, the one with a lustrous [...] *suh*-crown, the dragon of *Nijin-jar* (?), the queen of heaven and earth, Inanna, has erected a house in your precinct, *E.ana*, and taken her seat upon your dais. [...] the house of Inanna in *Unug*.

'House Where Lustrous Herbs are Strewn Upon the Flowery Bed', the bed-chamber of holy Inanna, where the lady of the plain refreshes herself! Brick-built *E.muc* ('House Which is the Precinct') is flowery and holy, its [...] clay established for him who tends the ewes on the high plain. Your [...] house of *Arali* ('House Which is the Nether World') gives shade to the shepherd. Your prince, a raging lion on the plain, the *cuba*-jewel of the 'Mistress Whose Breast is Holy and Marvelous', the lord who is holy Inanna's husband, *Dumuzi(d)* {*Tammuz*}, the sovereign of *E.muc*, has erected a house in your precinct, O *Bad-tibira*, and taken his seat upon your dais. [...] the house of *Dumuzi* in *Bad-tibira*.

E.igizu-uru ('House, With a Mighty Face'), with plenty coming from within, your well-stocked chamber is a mountain of abundance. House, your fragrance is a mound of vines. Your true minister is a leader in heaven. House, your princess is prominent among the gods, the true minister of *E.ana*, who holds a holy-sceptre in her hand. *Nincubur* {*Ninkubar*}, the true minister of *E.ana*, has erected a house in your precinct, O *E.akkil* ('house of lamentation'), and taken her seat upon your dais. [...] the house of *Nincubur* in *Akkil*.

O city, founded upon a dais in the *abzu*, established for the rites of *icib*-priests, house where incantations of heaven and earth are recited [...] [...] [...] lustration water in the holy heaven and on the pure earth. *Ningirim*, the lady of the shining lustration water, has erected a house in your precinct, O house *Murum*, and taken her seat upon your dais. [...] the house of *Ningirim* in *Murum*.

E.ninnu ('House of Fifty'), right hand of *Lagac*, foremost in *Sumer*; the *Anzu(d)*-bird which gazes upon the mountain, the *car-ur* weapon of [...] *Ninjirsu* {*Ningirsu*}; [...] in all lands, the strength of battle, a terrifying storm which envelops men, giving the strength of battle to the *Anuna* {*Anunnaki*}, the great gods; brick building on whose holy mound destiny is determined, beautiful as the hills, your canal [...], your [...] blowing in opposition at your gate facing towards *Iri-kug*, wine is poured into holy Anu's beautiful bowls set out in the open air. Whatever enters you is unequaled, whatever leaves endures. [...], terrifying facade, house of radiance, a place of reaching judgment which Lord *Ninjirsu* has filled with great awesomeness and dread! All the *Anuna* gods attend your great drinking-bouts.

Your prince, a raging storm which destroys cities in hostile lands, your sovereign, a terrifying wild ox which will manifest its strength, a terrifying lion which smashes heads, the warrior who devises strategies in lordship and attains victory in kingship, the mighty one, the great warrior in battle, the lord without rival, the son of Enlil, Lord *Ninjirsu*, has erected a house in your precinct, *E.ninnu*, and taken his seat upon your dais. [...] the house of *Ninjirsu* in *Lagac*.

O *Iri-kug* ('holy city'), shrine of holy Anu, which caused the human seed to come forth, called by a good name, within you is the river of ordeal which vindicates the just man. *E.jalga-sud* {*E.gal-ga-sud*} ('House Which Spreads Wisdom Far and Wide'), storehouse which eternally possesses silver and lapis lazuli; *E.tar-sirsir*, from which decisions and the divine powers come forth, where the hero performs obeisance, your princess, the merciful princess of the Land, is the mother of all lands. The lady, the great healer of the black-headed who determines the destiny of her city, the first-born daughter of holy Anu, the maiden, Mother Bau, has erected a house in your precinct, O house *Iri-kug* and taken her seat upon your dais. [...] the house of Bau in *Iri-kug*.

O house, wild cow [...], city which appears in splendor adorned for the princess, *Sirara*, great and princely place, your [...] by the shrine, your lady *Nance*, a great storm, a mighty flood, born on the shore of the sea, who laughs on the foam of the sea, who plays on the water of the flood, who [...], *Nance*, the [...] lady, has erected a house in your precinct, O house *Sirara*, and taken her seat upon your dais. [...] the house of *Nance* in

Sirara.

E.ab-caga-la ('House Which Stretches Over the Midst of the Sea') built in a holy place; *Gu-aba*, your interior produces everything and is a well-established storehouse. Holy shrine, wild cow for which everything endures, your princess is *Ninjagia* (?), the magnificent [...] stewardess, the mighty [...] of Father Enlil, who takes counsel with Lord Nunamnir. Born in [...], [...] in the flood of the sea, like her [...] father a controller of the pure sea, holy *Ninmarki* has erected a house in your precinct, O house *Gu-aba*, and taken her seat upon your dais. [...] the house of *Ninmarki* in *Gu-aba*.

O house *Kinirca*, suited for its lady, [...], beautiful as a hill, standing by the ziggurat, house, [...], place resounding loudly with happiness, house, your princess is a storm, riding on a lion, [...]. Exalted in holy song and antiphony, singing with a loud voice, the child, the true wild cow, taken care of at the holy breast of the mother who begot her, *Dumuzi-abzu*, has erected a house in your precinct, O shrine *Kinirca*, and taken her seat upon your dais. [...] the house of *Dumuzi-abzu* in *Kinirca*.

E.bur-sigsig ('House With Beautiful Bowls') set up under heaven, mighty banqueting hall, fulfilling the commands, abundance of the midst of the sea in [...], at whose holy [...] there is entreaty and joy. The faithful man has enlarged *E.mag* {*E.mah*} ('magnificent house'), the house of *Cara*, for you in plenty. Your house *E.mah*, whose prince is the princely son of the Mistress, continues in good fortune, an area of abundance and well-being. The one who arranges the hair at the nape of the neck, with the gaze of a wild cow, *Cara*, who [...] good things, the son who allots the divine powers to his mother, has erected a house in your precinct, O house *Umma*, and taken his seat upon your dais. [...] the house of *Cara* in *Umma*.

E.cerzi-guru ('House Dressed in Splendor'), dressed with ornaments of *cuba*-stone; great awesomeness, *Nijin-jar* (*Ningingar* ?) of holy Inanna, adorned throughout with the divine powers which are true; *Zabalam*, shrine of the shining mountain, shrine of [...] dawn, which has resounded with pleasure; the Mistress has founded your good banqueting hall for you in pleasure. Your Lady, Inanna, the [...], the singular woman, the dragon who speaks hostile words to [...], who shines in brightness, who goes against the rebel land, through whom the firmament is made beautiful in the evening, the great daughter of *Su-en* (*Nanna-Sin*), holy Inanna, has erected a house in your precinct, O house *Zabalam*, and taken her seat upon your dais. [...] the house of Inanna in *Zabalam*.

O 'House Inspiring Terror Like a Great Lion', making as clear as day the decisions for those on the high plain, house of *Ickur*, at your front is abundance, at your rear is celebration. Your foundation is a horned bull, a lion. Holy staff, teat of heaven with rain for fine barley, the pilasters of your house are a wild bull with outspread horns, your [...], foundation and wall rising high [...], thick cloud, [....] snake, [...] moonlight, [...] *Ickur*, a sweeping flood, [...] a storm and seven raging winds, [...], blowing raging winds, [...] running from the [...], splits the [...] hillside, diorite, stones and [...] [...] the seed of the Land, the [...], the [...] prince, the canal inspector of heaven and earth, the [...] living, the numerous people, the [...], *Ickur* has erected a house in your precinct, O house *Karkara*, and taken his seat upon your dais. [...] the house of *Ickur* in *Karkara*.

O [...], bolt founded by Anu, [...] [...] [...] [...] [...] has erected a house in your precinct, O [...], and taken a seat upon your dais. [...] the house of [...] in [....].

Anu has [...] your platform. *E.mah* ('exalted house'), 'House of the Universe', suited for its lady, your front inspires great awesomeness, your interior is filled with radiance. Mother *Nintur*, Enlil, and Enki have determined your destiny. *E.suga* ('joyous house') which [...], life of the black-haired people, Anu has given you the magnificent divine powers from the interior of heaven. As in *Kec*, *Ninhursag(a)* has blessed your priests maintaining the shrine in the holy *uzga*-precinct. 'House with Great Divine Powers', a pure platform and cleansing lustration; *Acgi* {*Akgi*}, the god of *Adab*, has erected a house in your precinct, *Adab*, house situated at a canal, and taken his seat upon your dais. [...] the house of *Ninhursag(a)* in *Adab*.

Isin, city founded by Anu, which he has built on an empty plain; Its front is mighty, its interior is artfully built, its divine powers are divine powers which An has determined. Shrine which Enlil loves, place where Anu and Enlil determine destinies, place where the great gods dine, filled with great awesomeness and terror: all the *Anuna* gods attend your great drinking-bouts. Your princess, the mother, the Mistress adorned with jewels of *cuba*-stone, who maintains the holy place's *Nijin-jar*, who binds the *suh*-crown on the *nugig*-priestess, who causes the seven teats to flow for the *nubar*-priestess, has resounded with seven pleasures. Your lady, the great healer of the Land, *Ninisina*, the daughter of Anu, has erected a house in your precinct, O house *Isin*, and taken her seat upon your dais. [...] the house of *Ninisina* in *Isin*.

Kazallu, your crown reaches to the center of

heaven, shining, [...] an object of admiration.
Your prince is the seed of a bull, engendered by
a wild bull in [...], a magnificent [...] with spark-
ling eyes, a lord with the teeth of a lion, who
snatches the calf with his claws, who snatches
[...] who snatches [...], the [...] who gives
strength to the [...], the great lord *Numucda*, has
erected a house in your precinct, O *Kun-satu*
('Threshold of the Mountain'), *Kazallu*, and taken
his seat upon your dais. [...] the house of *Numucda* in *Kazallu*.

E.igi-kalama ('House Which is the Eye of the
Land'), your foundation is firmly laid, growing
hill which stands broadly on the earth, [...] the
enemies' land, [...] [...] [...] has erected a house in
your precinct, O [...], and taken a seat upon your
dais. [...] the house of *Lugal-marda* in *Marda*.

Der {an archaic Akkadian name}, taking extreme
care of decisions, [...], on your awesome and radiant gate a decoration displays a horned viper
and a *muchuc* embracing {seized in a trap}. Your
prince, a leader of the gods, fit for giving counsel and grand speech, the son of *Urac* who knows
thoroughly the true divine powers of princeship, *Ictaran* the [...] sovereign of heaven, has
erected a house in your precinct, *E.dim-gal-
kalama* ('House Which is the Great Pole/Axis of
the Land'), and taken his seat upon your dais.
[...] the house of *Ictaran* in *Der*.

O *E.sikil* ('pure house') whose pure divine powers are supreme in all lands, whose name is high and mighty, magnificent dwelling of the warrior, holy house of *Ninazu*, house of the holy divine powers! House, your divine powers are pure divine powers, your lustration is a cleansing lustration. The warrior refreshes himself in your dwelling. *Ninazu* dines on your platform. Your sovereign, the great lord, the son of Enlil, is a towering lion spitting venom over hostile lands, rising like the south wind against enemy lands, snarling like a dragon against the walls of rebel lands, a storm enveloping the disobedient and trampling on the enemy. When he strides forth, no evil-doer can escape. When he establishes his triumph, the cities of the rebel lands are destroyed. When he frowns, their people are cast into the dust. House, your prince is a great lion from whose claws the enemy hangs. Your sovereign is a terrifying, mighty storm, the vigor of the battle, in combat [...] like a [...] with a shield on his lofty arm, a net over the widespread people from whose reach the foe cannot escape. When the great lord is resplendent, his magnificence has no equal. The true seed born of the Great Mountain and Ninlil, your sovereign, the warrior *Ninazu*, has erected a house in your precinct, O *E.sikil*, O *Ecnunna*, and taken his seat upon your dais. [...] the house of *Ninazu* in *Ecnunna*.

'House Built in Plenitude', *Kic*, raising its head among the princely divine powers, established settlement, your great foundation cannot be scattered. Your plinth is a vast oppressive cloud floating in the midst of the sky. Your interior is a weapon, a mace decorated with [...]; Your right hand makes mountains tremble, your left thins out the enemy. Your prince, mighty and magnificent, a great storm overpowering the earth, inspiring great and terrifying awe, your sovereign, the warrior *Zababa*, has erected a house in your precinct, O *E.dub* ('storage house'), O house *Kic*, and taken his seat upon your dais. [...] the house of *Zababa* in *Kic*.

E.kecda-kalama ('House Which is the Bond of the Land'), bull [...] great strength among the gods, terrifying wild cow, wild bull which causes lament; *Gudua*, your quay is a low quay which bestows water, your interior is artfully built, your mace is a [...] mace released from heaven, your platform is a lustrous platform spreading over *Mec-lam* {'Underworld'}. Your prince, the mighty god, the sovereign of *Mec-lam*, the fierce god of the underworld, the sovereign of *Ud-cuc* {sunset}, *Nergal*, *Mec-lam(ta)-ea*, has erected a house in your precinct, and taken his seat upon your dais. [...] the house of *Nergal* in *Gudua*.

O mighty *Urum* where *Su-en* (*Nanna-Sin*) pronounces judgment; *E.ab-lua* ('House With

Teeming Cattle'), wide cattle-yard, *Acimbabbar*
acts as your shepherd. House, my sovereign,
your sceptre reaches to heaven, [...] to the earth,
moonlight [...], celebration, your [...] may [...]
the light. Your prince, the prince of holy celebration, [...], who appears in the lapis lazuli
colored sky, a celebration, to whom the hero
pays homage [...], who brightens the Land, [...].
Su-en, has erected a house in your precinct, O
house *Urum* and taken his seat upon your dais.
[...] the house of *Su-en* in *Urum*.

Zimbir, dais upon which *Utu* (*Shammash*) sits
daily, *E.nun-ana* ('House of the Prince of
Heaven'), star of heaven, crown given birth by
Ningal, house of *Utu*, your prince, the [...] of the
universe, fills heaven and earth. When the lord
sleeps, the people sleep; when he rises, the
people rise. The bull [...] and the people prostrate themselves. Before *Utu* the herds pasture
[...]. The black-haired humans have bathed before him, the Land has [...] before him. He
measures out the divine powers; your shrine is a
flood. Pronouncing judgment where the sun
rises, mighty sunlight, wearing a beard, tying on
the *suh*-crown at night, *Utu*, the sovereign of
E.Babbar ('shining house'), has erected a house in
your precinct, O house *Zimbir*, and taken his seat
upon your dais. [...] the house of *Utu* in *Zimbir*.

E.hursag ('House Which is a Mountain') beautiful as greenery, [...] your interior is plenitude. At the place where destiny is determined, you determine destiny. May the crown bring joy to your platform. May your roots glisten like an immense *sajkal*-snake in your holy foundations. Mother *Nintur*, the lady of creation, performs her task within your dark place, binding the true *suh*-crown on the new-born king, setting the crown on the new-born lord who is secure in her hand. The midwife of heaven and earth, *Ninhursag(a)*, has erected a house in your precinct, O house [...], and taken her seat upon your dais. [...] the house of *Ninhursag(a)* in [...].

O *Ulmac*, upper land, [...] of the Land, terrifying lion battering a wild bull, net spreading over an enemy, making silence fall upon a rebel land on which, as long as it remains insubmissive, spittle is poured! House of Inanna {*or* Ishtar} of silver and lapis lazuli, a storehouse built of gold, your princess is an *arabu*-bird, the Mistress of the *Nijin*-jar. Arrayed in battle, jubilantly beautiful, ready with the seven maces, washing her tools for battle, opening the door of battle and [...], the extremely wise one of heaven, Inanna has erected a house in your precinct, O house *Ulmac*, and taken her seat upon your dais. [...] the house of Inanna of *Ulmac*.

O house [...], right arm, battle-axe cutting down the rebel lands, digging up their green fields,

[...] [...] Your prince, the warrior who [...], who defeats all in battle, exulting [...], *Aba*, the god of *Agade* {*Akkad*}, has erected a house in your precinct, O house *Agade*, and taken his seat upon your dais. [...] the house of *Aba* in *Agade*.

'House of Stars', bright *E.zagin-guna* ('House Dressed in Lapis Lazuli'), reaching into all lands, establishing [...] in the shrine, *Eresh*. The primeval lords raise their heads to you every month. [...] the potash plant, great *Nanibgal*, *Nisaba* {*Teshmet*} has brought divine powers from heaven and added to your divine powers. Sanctuary established for [...]! To the true woman who possesses exceeding wisdom, soothing [...] and opening the mouth, always consulting a Tablet-of-Lapis-Lazuli, giving advice to all lands, the true woman, the holy potash plant, born of the stylus-reed, applies the measure to heaven and places the measuring-rope on the earth, to Nisaba, be praised! The compiler of the tablets was *En-hedu-ana* {presumably *Nabu*}. My king, something has been created that no one has created before. [...] the house of *Nisaba* in *Eresh*.

'BEFORE ALL BEFORES'
(*Ancient Poetic Hymn of Creation*)

Before all befores, there was Nammu, she the origin, ever flowing beginning. Nammu was the first, the source, the mother of the universe, the self-procreating womb of abundance, alone and all-in-one; Nammu was primal matter, the deep fertile waters of the sea.

Before all befores, for time was yet to be; Nammu revolved and flowed, squeezed, coiled, and rushed like a double-helix spiral. Nammu's waters then opened up: she had given birth to Ki-An, creation's first born; she the mountain, he the sky.

Before all befores, wrapped around the liquid body of the mother, Ki the mountain, An the sky held each other close in a most tender embrace. Ki the mountain, An the sky lay in each other's arms before all befores; when An was an empty sky, Ki a stony earth, laying barren and unfulfilled within Nammu's fecund body fluid as Ki and An lay closer still, something stirred, deep from within.

Love that bound An and Ki together brought into being a sigh, a wind, a first breath; and so was Enlil, Infant Lord Air, manifested. Thus, life throbbed in cheerful continuation, as An, the mighty bull of heaven, made love fifty times (and more) to Ki, his beloved, the all-powerful cow of earth.

Ki responded to An's enthusiasm and passion in kind. She made herself resplendent; for (her brother-spouse) she beautified her body with the most precious metals, fuels and lapis lazuli; she adorned herself with diorite, chalcedony and shiny carnelian. So did the skyfather An array himself in a cloak of purest azure to greet his dearest Ki.

Then in great joy and reverence An, who called himself heaven then, approached Ki, whom he called earth. An-heaven dived into Ki's welcoming expanse. Then (sky) kissed Ki, pouring the semen of trees, reeds and pastures into the beloved's womb.

Ki, fecund, brave, sweet earth, was impregnated with the rich semen of heaven, and joyfully gave birth to the planets of life. Luxuriantly did Earth bear the rich produce, generously did she exude wine and honey.

Gleefully, she invited the skies into herself over and over again. Fifty times (and more), sky came into the earth. Fifty times (and more), An's seed met Ki; fifty times (and more), An's seed grew in Ki; fifty times (and more), An and Ki made love; and so the Anunnaki, in Ki's womb was formed, as yet unnamed, waiting to be born.

Only Enlil, Infant Lord Air was there within An's and Ki's lap, all surrounded by Nammu's depths. Nammu feels and sees everything. She must now create space for her offspring. Under Ki, surrounding Enlil, above An, Nammu arches and stretches her watery form; to further depths, she directs.

Nammu defines herself as the first ocean, cradle of other life forms to come. "Mine are the depths reaching out to the surface," decrees (the fates) Nammu; "Mine is the process of becoming out of nothing's embrace. Mine is the nurturing womb, life's first mystery; Mine is the silence that all life created."

'LOVE SONG OF NABU & TESHMET'

The fragrance of cedar is your love, O lord! The shade of the cedar, the king's shelter. His stature is like Lebanon, select as the cedars. How gorgeous she is, how resplendent! Tašmetu, looking exuberant, enters the bedroom. How beautiful you are, my darling, how beautiful!

Rejoice, Nanaya, in the garden of Ebabbar that you love! Let my Tašmetu come with me to the garden. I have come to my garden, my sister and bride.

By night I thought of you. She got onto the bed, into a bowl her tears flow. On my bed at night I missed him whom I love. After I lay in the bosom of the son, Tašmetu fondles a bunch of gold in the lap of Nabû. A bundle of myrrh is my lover to me, between my breasts he lies.

A quarter of you is lapis lazuli. Whose whole being is a tablet of lapis lazuli. His belly is a plaque
of ivory overlaid with lapis lazuli. Come and rejoice, O king! Let me make you happy in the
tablet house! Bring me to your chamber, O king!

⁂ APPENDIX A ⁂
COSMIC LAW (ARCANE TABLETS)*

The *Arcane Tablets* reveal that the *Cosmos* is regulated by a "Cosmic Law"—actually *Seven Cosmic Laws*—superimposed over the *Universe*.

I. *The Law of Orderly Trend.*
"Under this law, there is always manifested law and order in the Cosmos, from suns to atoms; from the highest to the lowest; matter, energy and consciousness."

II. *The Law of Analogy.*
"Under this law, there is found a correspondence and agreement between all of the various forms of manifestation. What is true of the atom, is true of the sun. What is true of matter, is true of energy and mind. To know one is to know all."

III. *The Law of Sequence.*
"Under this law, there is included the activities of what is generally known as 'cause and effect'. Nothing in existence happens by pure chance. Nothing happens without a precedent manifestation, and a subsequent manifestation. Nothing stands alone in exclusion."

IV. *The Law of Rhythm.*
"Under this law falls a variety of phenomena, the most important of which is 'vibration'. Everything

---

* Excerpted from "*Fundamentals of Systemology.*"

in existence is in constant vibration—everything material, mental, or of 'energy'. Upon this fact depends the variety, degrees, states, and conditions, of the manifestations in the Cosmos. To control vibration is to control all forces in the Universe."

V. *The Law of Balance.*

"Under this law, there is to be found an explanation for the universal equilibrium, compensation, and balance, observed in all manifestation in the Cosmos. One thing balances another; everything has something set opposite it, to balance it."

VI. *The Law of Cyclicity.*

"Under this law is found the cyclic—or circular—trend of all things, physical, mental and spiritual. Everything moves in circular systems. The wise convert the circles into upward spirals. Instead of traveling and endless circle, or downward, the wise rise in spirals to attainment and advancement."

VII. *The Law of Opposites.*

"Under this law is an explanation of the fact that everything has its opposite; everything is and is-not at the same time; everything has its other side —also the fact that opposite things are alike, in the end, for the extremes meet and contradiction may be reconciled."

.: APPENDIX B :.
ENUMA ELISH (SUMMARY)

TABLET I.

a.)—ABZU (*the Abyss*) and TIAMAT (*the Cosmic Dragon*) are first forms; form the One (*All*).

b.)—Generations of "gods" are born and begin to make too much noise.

c.)—TIAMAT entrusts her vizier KINGU the power to fight for her.

d.)—TIAMAT creates calamity and a horde of monsters as ammunition.

TABLET II.

a.)—Enki reveals the plot against the gods to ANSAR.

b.)—A primary discourse from Tablet-I is repeated.

TABLET III.

a.)—Anu, Enlil and Enki do not stand fit to battle against TIAMAT.

b.)—Marduk is petitioned to champion the Anunnaki gods.

c.)—Marduk asks for supreme divinity if successful; to be *Chief God*.

TABLET IV.

a.)—The Anunnaki agree to Marduk's terms and prepare him for battle.

b.)—Marduk receives a "cloak of invisibility."

c.)—Marduk enchants his favored weapon: a bow.

d.)—Marduk destroys KINGU with a thunderbolt.

e.)—TIAMAT is slain; her minions are scattered and sent to "secret places."

f.)—Marduk fashions a "*Gate*" to seal these energies separate from the material universe

TABLET V.

a.)—Marduk seals the cosmic systems of "Lights," "Spheres" and "Degrees" under himself.

b.)—A material-matix *below* is fragmented by "seven," while the *heights* remain divided into "twelve."

c.)—The "*Anunnaki Star-Gate*" system is sealed throughout the Universe.

d.)—Marduk sets up a throne for himself next to Anu.

TABLET VI.

a.)—The Anunnaki praise Marduk for his feats.

b.)—The "Key to the Gate" (of the *Abyss* or *Dragon*) is "hidden" in genetic memory of the "*Race of Marduk*," including humans upgraded by Enki.

c.)—Babylonian systematization begins.

TABLET VII.

a.)—Having slayed TIAMAT and granted power over material creation, Marduk takes fifty names and the "number" of Enlil.

b.)—Marduk takes the "signs" and esoteric knowledge ("magic") of Enki.

c.)—Marduk fractures then seals all systems on Earth under his name.

MARDUKITE
MASTER COURSE

Experience the Legendary "Complete Mardukite Master Course" exactly as given in person by Joshua Free to the "Mardukite Academy of Systemology" in September 2020.

Transcripts to all 48 Course Lectures + Instructor's Manual

Over 800 pages of material collected in one huge hardcover textbook anthology.

This volume references 25 years of chronological research, development and publishing, spanning *Mardukite Academy Grade-I, II & III*, covering material presented in Master Grade textbooks:

"The Great Magickal Arcanum,"

"Merlyn's Complete Book of Druidism,"

"Necronomicon: Complete Anunnaki Legacy,"

and *"The Systemology Handbook."*

THE FUNDAMENTALS OF
SYSTEMOLOGY

A Basic Course by
Joshua Free

*collecting material from all six lesson-booklets
together in one volume!*

"Being More Than Human"

"Realities in Agreement"

"Windows To Experience"

"Ancient Systemology"

"A History of Systemology"

"Systemology Processing"

All *six* lesson-booklets of the first official
New Standard Systemology Basic Course
are combined together in *one volume* as
"Fundamentals of Systemology."

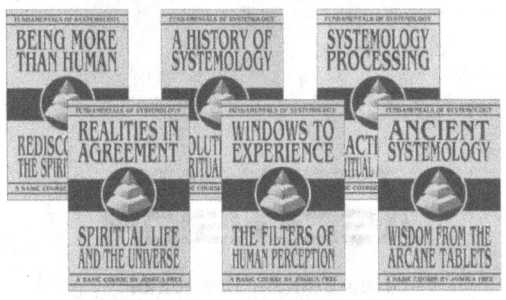

All 6 lesson-booklets also available individually!

Collector's Edition Hardcover

THE PATHWAY TO
ASCENSION

The New Standard Systemology
Professional Course by
Joshua Free

All 16 lessons available in two hardcover volumes!

"Increasing Awareness"

"Thought & Emotion"

"Clear Communication"

"Handling Humanity"

"Free Your Spirit"

"Escaping Spirit-Traps"

"Eliminating Barriers"

"Conquest of Illusion"

...and more!

All *sixteen* lesson-booklets of the official
New Standard Professional Course
combined together in *two hardcover volumes*
or *one oversized paperback workbook* as
"The Pathway to Ascension."

All lesson-booklets are also available individually!

PUBLISHED BY THE **JOSHUA FREE** IMPRINT REPRESENTING

The Founding Church of Mardukite Zuism

THE JOSHUA FREE IMPRINT
JFI PUBLICATIONS

MARDUKITE
ZUISM

mardukite.com